A New View
Of AD/HD

A NEW VIEW
OF AD/HD

SUCCESS STRATEGIES FOR THE IMPULSIVE LEARNER

Eric Jensen

with

Karen Markowitz • Michael Dabney
Karen Selsor • Jennifer Decker Arevalo

CORWIN PRESS
A SAGE Publications Company
Thousand Oaks, CA 91320

For information:

Corwin Press
A SAGE Publications Company
2455 Teller Road
Thousand Oaks, California 91320
www.corwinpress.com

SAGE Publications India Pvt. Ltd.
B 1/I 1 Mohan Cooperative Industrial Area
Mathura Road, New Delhi 110 044
India

SAGE Publications Ltd.
1 Oliver's Yard
55 City Road
London EC1Y 1SP
United Kingdom

SAGE Publications Asia-Pacific Pte. Ltd.
33 Pekin Street #02-01
Far East Square
Singapore 048763

Printed in the United States of America.

ISBN: 978-1-8904-6023-5

This book is printed on acid-free paper.

07 08 09 10 11 9 8 7 6 5 4 3 2 1

Note of Caution: Human behavior is an ever-changing science. New research and technology, better medications and treatments, and more effective interventions are constantly emerging. This being said, the author and publisher of this book have checked facts with multiple reliable sources to ensure accuracy and industry-standard reliability. Nevertheless, human error does occur and ever-changing advancements can deem information outdated very quickly. Therefore, the author and publisher cannot warrant the information herein, the only, the best, or the most current available at the time of reading.

The author/publisher encourage readers to consult multiple sources before taking action, particularly when dealing with chronic, debilitating, and dangerous disorders. A response team that includes teacher, student, parents, a school administrator, nurse, resource specialist, or counselor, and the child's physician/health professional is typically the best option. The author and publisher cannot accept responsibility or liability for either the accuracy or application of the information presented in this book. When it comes to medications and treating serious disorders, deficits, or learning disabilities, always consult a team of professionals including your physician, psychiatrist, counselor, and other qualified caregivers.

AD/HD is a constellation of context-dependent behaviors most disruptive in restricted environments. But in the right environment, it is no more a disability than being blind in the dark or being dyslexic on the soccer field.

Table of Contents

1

A New Revolutionary View of AD/HD

Attention-Deficit/Hyperactivity Disorder (AD/HD) does *not* meet the established medical criteria for a *disease*. Nor does it have the life cycle of one (DSM IV-TR 2000). Although commonly referred to as a *disorder*, AD/HD is really a constellation of *context-dependent behaviors* that are most prevalent in very constrictive environments. In other words, most people with AD/HD function just fine in casual settings, including the majority of home and recreational environments. These learners, however, are likely to experience some challenges in highly structured, less flexible environments like school or places of worship.

This realization is important because it recognizes that the most complex organ in our body, our brain, cannot accurately be understood in terms of black or white, good or bad, fixed or broken. Rather, AD/HD entails many shades of "impairment" depending on factors such as degree of classroom structure, teaching style, and a child's own ability to accommodate for differences. When viewed like this, we realize that AD/HD characteristics can be a gift! In fact, most AD/HD learners who are provided with positive learning experiences go on to lead successful lives as adults and make productive contributions to their community.

Former professional basketball player Dennis Rodman, for example, has had consistent problems with social conformity, but on the court his impulsivity made him an NBA All-Star. Paul Orfalea, founder of Kinko's copy shops, graduated near the bottom of his high-school class, but in the fast-paced business world, his AD/HD turned out to be a gift.

Despite their differences, many teachers love the diversity their AD/HD learners bring to the classroom and find, in many cases, they are more interesting and engaging than their average students. When differences are channeled, accommodated, and embraced rather than resisted, a productive and positive learning environment always results.

This different spin on AD/HD is not meant to minimize the problem or ignore its impact on learners and the classroom, but to more accurately define the challenge it presents. Some leaders in educational reform have pointed out that the *negative aspects* of AD/HD are what usually get emphasized, when in fact some AD/HD characteristics resemble those of highly creative, divergent thinkers identified as "gifted and talented" (Leroux & Levitt-Perlman 2000).

Name Change Reflects More Precise Definition

As our understanding of AD/HD has evolved over the past 50 years, so has our definition of it. The American Psychiatric Association's *Diagnostic and Statistics Manual IV* (DSM-IV TR 2000) recently revised the previously used acronyms ADD and ADHD to AD/HD. This occurred because time has revealed that AD/HD most commonly includes both the inattention component *and* the hyperactivity-impulsive component; however, some individuals exhibit one or the other predominantly. Thus, AD/HD includes three subtypes: (1) Attention-Deficit/ Hyperactivity Disorder - Combined Type (the most prevalent); (2) Attention-Deficit/Hyperactivity Disorder - Predominantly Inattentive; and (3) Attention-Deficit/Hyperactivity Disorder - Predominantly Hyperactive-Impulsive Type.

Attention-Deficit/Hyperactivity Disorder

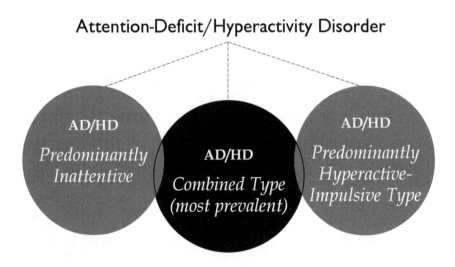

AD/HD
Predominantly
Inattentive

AD/HD
Combined Type
(most prevalent)

AD/HD
Predominantly
Hyperactive-
Impulsive Type

This change suggests that AD/HD is a spectrum event: Brain system dysfunctions that lead to one "misbehavior" also lead to others. Reduced frontal-lobe activation, for example, will result in working-memory deficits, temporal-processing deficiencies, and impulse dysregulation. In combination, these anomalies lead to hyperactivity, inattention, and impulsivity—the classic AD/HD symptoms.

Symptoms of AD/HD

AD/HD is characterized by four primary symptoms: (1) Achronica (temporal-processing deficits); (2) Disinhibition (impulsivity and reward aversion); (3) Working-memory deficits (delay aversion); and (4) Hyperactivity (arousal activation dysfunction). It is easy to generalize and say that a child who exhibits hyperactivity or inattention or both is AD/HD. For an accurate AD/HD diagnosis, however, the DSM IV (2000) suggests that all of the following criteria must be met:

1. **The symptoms or behaviors appear before age seven.**
2. **The symptoms or behaviors last at least six months.**
3. **The level of disturbance is more severe and frequent than age norms.**
4. **The behaviors create a real handicap in at least two areas of the individual's life (i.e., school, home, social settings).**

Although the condition is not classified as a *learning* disability, the symptoms make it difficult for many to perform well in school. The inherent behavioral challenges of the condition combined with AD/HD's prevalence, make it an issue of intense concern for educators today.

A Contextual Condition, But Definitely Real!

Some skeptics question whether AD/HD is real: This is like asking if introversion is real. Absolutely! AD/HD represents a clearly established behavioral profile that can either be a good or bad fit depending on the environment. In roles, for example, that do not require sustained short-term memory, restraint, or judgments of timing, the AD/HD student often excels. And AD/HD adults with control over their own scheduling and work-style, are usually very successful. Although not necessarily suited for extremely routine tasks or high-stakes roles like meticulous assembly-line work or the fine-print detail required of attorneys, there are many artists, entrepreneurs, fire fighters, factory workers, and classroom teachers that are AD/HD.

A blind student has no disability in the dark; a dyslexic is not disadvantaged on the soccer field; the AD/HD student succeeds in high-choice environments.

An artist's brain is different than a salesperson's brain, and a contractor's brain is going to be different than a college professor's brain. Experience and genes play a role in shaping the anatomical subtleties in the brain, as well as chemical balance. So, while real biological differences exist, *how important they are is contextually dependent.* In other words, the AD/HD student's experience in school may be positive or negative depending on the environment he/she encounters there.

Variations Exist in the AD/HD Brain

There are anatomical, functional, and chemical variations in the AD/HD brain that are associated with weak temporal processing, delay aversion, and short-term memory dysfunction. But these variations are not 100% consistent or significant. Although the condition has biological correlates, AD/HD cannot be defined or diagnosed merely by an EEG reading or other brain-imaging device. Brain scans often show differences in the brains of individuals with AD/HD; however, a causal relationship has not been established. Rather, researchers emphasize that differences in experience, lifestyle, occupation, education, and/or environment change the brain accordingly. Distress, for example, over time causes neuronal death as does chronic threat, agitation, and neglect.

Although the exact cause of AD/HD is still unclear, there is strong evidence that a deficiency in the neurotransmitter dopamine may be a chemical basis for the condition (Ding, et al. 2002). It is clear that AD/HD tends to run in families and recent genetic studies support an 80% heredity factor (Faraone & Doyle 2000; Smalley 1997). However, not everyone diagnosed with AD/HD has the same brain variations or constellation of symptoms.

2   *Who Really Has It?*

AD/HD is the most commonly diagnosed behavioral condition in school-age children. Researchers at the Mayo Clinic recently studied 8,000 children and determined that the lowest estimate of school-age children diagnosed with AD/HD is 7.5% and the highest is 17% (Barbaresi, et al. 2002). Previous reports, using less stringent research criteria, estimated that as many as 20% of children had AD/HD; other reports estimate that only 3% of school-aged children are affected, a figure since deemed too low. Studies, which include America's adult population, suggest that 15 to 20 million Americans of all ages may have AD/HD (Barbaresi, et al. 2002).

Boys are diagnosed with the condition three to eight times more often than girls and Caucasians twice as often as African Americans. Many of the children diagnosed with AD/HD are under the age of four. Reports indicate that 57% are being treated with at least one drug. Some evidence suggests that 80% of pediatric visits for AD/HD result in a stimulant prescription. Prescription medications are three times more likely to be used in the treatment of boys than girls, and as AD/HD sufferers age, the use of med-  ication increases. One study reported that by the fifth grade, 20% of Caucasian boys were taking a medication for AD/HD, and some middle schools reported as many as 50%.

The AD/HD student's experience in school may be positive or negative depending on the environment he/she encounters.

Since 1990, the total number of American students diagnosed with AD/HD has increased from almost one million to nearly six million (see Graph below), and the use of stimulant medications (such as Ritalin/Concerta and Adderall) has increased 700% in the same period.

The Growing Prevalence/Diagnosis of AD/HD

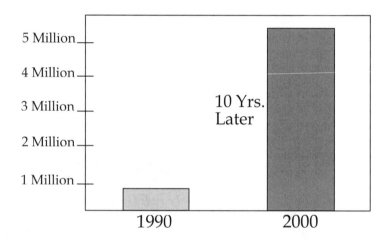

Since 1990, the total number of American children diagnosed with AD/HD has risen from 900,000 to over 5.5 million, and the use of stimulant medication has increased 700% in the same period.

There is no single known cause for AD/HD and the search for genetic markers has yielded inconclusive or modest effects. It has become clear from a search of the literature, however, that both environmental and genetic factors contribute to the etiology of this complex condition. Although the factors on the following page seem to put children at greater risk for AD/HD, they do not, alone, *cause* it.

AD/HD Risk Factors

- Genes: Family history of AD/HD
- Family history of alcoholism
- Antisocial male relatives
- Female relatives with Briquet's syndrome (hysteria/imagined illness)
- Living in poverty
- Being male
- Maternal smoking
- Family psychosocial adversity
- Severe problems in family relationships; divorce
- Child abuse or neglect
- Mental retardation
- Conduct disorders
- Low birth weight/Premature birth
- Traumatic brain injuries
- Sleep problems during infancy
- Prenatal exposure to alcohol, drugs, and/or nicotine
- Childhood lead poisoning

Due to the multiple uncertainties involved, parents and teachers should not attempt to diagnose AD/HD, but seek the opinion of a health-care professional if it is suspected. A family doctor can determine whether the child should be referred to a specialist, such as a developmental pediatrician, child psychiatrist, or developmental neurologist. If AD/HD is left untreated or misdiagnosed, it can have long-term adverse effects on academic, social, and emotional well-being—consequences usually avoided with the appropriate intervention.

Underdiagnosed or Overdiagnosed?

Intense debate continues as to whether the condition is over-diagnosed, but based on a review of studies from 1975 through March 1997, the American Medical Association or AMA (1999) reported there is little evidence of widespread over-diagnosis, misdiagnosis, or widespread over-prescribing of medications to treat AD/HD. In fact, the report claims "the symptoms of AD/HD, the degrees of impairment, and the course of the condition form a coherent pattern that enables well-trained clinicians to reliably diagnose the condition."

Despite the AMA's findings, there is concern among parents, educators, and health professionals regarding the alarmingly high and growing diagnosis of AD/HD, and the related problem of inappropriate use of potentially addictive stimulant medications for *mild* forms of the condition or as a first line of treatment.

What experts do agree on, however, is that the appropriate protocol for treating AD/HD is first an accurate diagnosis, second a compatible/ flexible environment, third behavioral therapy, and lastly medication, *if necessary*. AD/HD should be monitored closely and taken seriously. Although treatable, more serious problems generally ensue if ignored.

Growing Up with AD/HD

Contrary to popular belief, AD/HD is not outgrown. Up to 6% of the total adult population continues to exhibit AD/HD symptoms (Wender, et al. 2001). The rise in adults diagnosed with AD/HD has been attributed to the fact that parents become more educated about the condition after taking their child in for evaluation and begin to identify the symptoms in themselves. It is also likely that some adults have found ways to self-medicate, adapt, or otherwise choose occupations where job performance is minimally impacted by their condition. Overall, adults tend to have less hyperactivity, but more inattention and restlessness (Phalen 2002).

A 14-month study of 579 children with AD/HD, randomly assigned to different types of treatment, concluded that a combined treatment approach of medication and behavioral therapy was superior to behavioral therapy alone (MTA 1999). "But this does not mean that behavioral therapy has no role in treating AD/HD," the researchers report. More than three-fourths of subjects given behavioral treatment were successfully maintained without medication throughout the study, so it should *not* be concluded that behavioral treatment interventions are ineffective. Although researchers are still determining the effects of AD/HD in adults, most agree that through training, life adjustments, and accommodation, many individuals with AD/HD ultimately lead satisfying lives and successful careers.

Using a meticulous recruitment and screening/diagnostic process involving structured psychiatric interviews, investigators examined the functioning of 149 adults clinically referred and diagnosed as having AD/HD (Millstein, et al. 1998). The sample included 88 males and 61 females, and had a mean age of 37 years. They found that 56% of the adults had the combined subtype, 37% had the inattentive subtype, and only 2% had the hyperactive/impulsive subtype. Symptoms of inattention were the most commonly reported—particularly problems with sustaining attention, frequent shifts, and follow through. Hyperactive and impulsive symptoms were less common, but nonetheless the majority of the adults reported long-standing difficulties with fidgeting, interrupting, speaking out of turn, and impatience. Hyperactive/impulsive symptoms were reported to have decreased more from childhood to adulthood than inattentive symptoms.

In the study (ibid), comorbidity was very common. Only 3% had no comorbidity; 11% had a lifetime history of one comorbid condition; 12% had two; 18% had three; and 56% had four or more psychiatric comorbidities (ibid). Adults with the combined subtype tended to have more comorbid psychiatric conditions, particularly oppositional-defiant disorder, bipolar disorder, and substance-use disorders, than those with the inattentive or hyperactive/ impulsive subtype.

This study reinforces previous research in children showing that the combined subtype of AD/HD is the most common, and the hyperactive/ impulsive subtype is the least common. It also reinforces previous findings that the inattentive symptoms persist more than the hyperactive/ impulsive symptoms into adulthood, and provides valuable information about the types of comorbidities present in adults with AD/HD.

Curran and colleagues (1999) found a high percentage of the prison population has AD/HD (9% of prisoners vs. 2.5% of young adults in the general population). Clure and colleagues (1999) found that among inpatients for substance-use disorder (alcohol and/or cocaine use), 32% met the criteria for AD/HD, and 35% of those inpatients had a childhood diagnosis of AD/HD with symptoms continuing into adulthood.

Gender Differences In AD/HD

In another study involving 360 AD/HD patients, Arcia and Conners (1998) examined gender differences in intellectual ability, neuropsychological performance, and self-ratings of AD/HD symptoms and other behavioral and emotional problems. Their sample included 280 males and 80 females, ages 5 to 60. The researchers found that there were no differences between males and females at any age on the IQ tests, the Conners' Continuous Performance Test, or the Rey-Osterrieth Complex  Figure Test. Thus, on objective measures of intellectual ability and neuropsychological functioning, males and females were similar. There were no differences between male and female children on either parent or teacher rating scales; however, significant differences were measured between males and females on the self-ratings.

Compared to the males, female adolescents and adults with AD/HD rated themselves as having *fewer* assets, *more* problems of concentration, *more* problems of restlessness, *more* problems dealing with anger, *less* self-confidence, *more* emotional problems with feelings such as anxiety and depression, and *more* conflicts with their families (ibid).

In another study, Rucklidge and Kaplan (1998) investigated the psychological functioning of 51 women diagnosed as having AD/HD compared to 51 not fulfilling criteria for AD/HD. The women in both groups averaged 41 years of age. The investigators used a variety of interview and self-report measures to compare the AD/HD and non-AD/HD women on psychiatric history, depression, anxiety, life stresses, coping styles, and self-esteem. Women with AD/HD reported having had more depressive episodes in their lives, lower self-esteem, more feelings of anxiety, higher levels of stress, and more frequent involvement in psychotherapy than women without AD/HD. The AD/HD group also engaged in *less* task-oriented coping and *more* emotional coping and had a more *external* locus of control than the non-AD/HD group (e.g. felt they had less control over their lives).

Men with AD/HD, however, experience higher rates of conduct disorder, antisocial personality disorder, alcohol and drug dependence, and stuttering than women, but women with AD/HD experience higher rates of depression, bulimia nervosa, and simple phobias. Because of this high rate of comorbidity, the risk for misdiagnosis and undiscovered problems is very high.

Accommodation Tips

✏ Rather than asking AD/HD learners to stop doing something, redirect them towards an appropriate activity.

✏ Take advantage of school programs like "Study Buddies," Tutoring, and other outside family support networks.

✏ Use visual and non-verbal cues to communicate with AD/HD learners. Be very direct at first so that your cues are clearly understood.

✏ Look for signs of stress build up and provide encouragement, support and reduced workload, if necessary, to alleviate pressure.

✏ Use calming strategies to mitigate outbursts of temper. Do not punish, rather redirect and help the child communicate verbally versus becoming physical.

3

The New Biology of AD/HD

AD/HD arises from a frustrating and complex constellation of anatomical anomalies, brain malfunction, and chemical dysregulation. The two primary brain systems involved are the frontal lobes and the catecholaminergic (neurotransmitters) system. For a Working Model of AH/HD see Appendix I on page 61.

Executive Functions of the Frontal Lobes

The most common symptoms of AD/HD are associated with dysfunction in the frontal lobes and/or prefrontal cortex, which robs the brain of important cognitive elements such as self-control and attention. The frontal lobes control (among other things) temporal processing, impulsivity, working memory, and reward/delay aversion. Any significant deficits (i.e., head trauma, drug abuse, violence, or genetic aberration) will weaken this area of the brain and its ability to inhibit inappropriate behaviors, wait for rewards, and regulate thinking and memory. In fact, research reveals that typically the AD/HD student will choose an immediate reward when given the choice of double the reward after 30 seconds or an *immediate* reward within 5 seconds (Sonuga-Barke 2002).

Brain Areas Affected by AD/HD

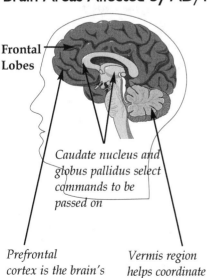

Frontal Lobes

Caudate nucleus and globus pallidus select commands to be passed on

Prefrontal cortex is the brain's command center

Vermis region helps coordinate actions

What Goes Wrong

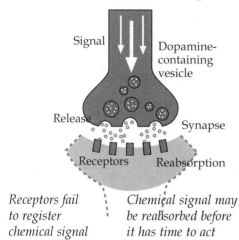

Signal

Dopamine-containing vesicle

Release

Synapse

Receptors Reabsorption

Receptors fail to register chemical signal

Chemical signal may be reabsorbed before it has time to act

Catecholaminergic Dysfunction

Catecholaminergic dysfunction (or chemical dysregulation) primarily influences arousal levels and is correlated with "spaced-out" behaviors and lack of attentiveness. The catecholimines include dopamine, epinephrine (adrenaline) and norepinephrine (noradrenaline). These common neurotransmitters provide the "horsepower" to manage the brain's executive functions.

Scientists believe that AD/HD may have strong genetic underpinnings, but non-genetic factors, such as premature birth, prenatal drug exposure, and maternal tobacco use, have also been linked to the condition. Although a single clear cause of AD/HD has not been identified, it is *not* directly related to poor parenting, too much television, or poor diet. These factors may exacerbate AD/HD, but they do not *cause* it. The following factors reflect the prevailing theories on the causes of AD/HD:

Heredity

Recent research suggests that some individuals inherit a biochemical condition that influences the expression of AD/HD symptoms. Genetic researchers in five different studies have discovered a link between a gene called the DRD4 repeater gene and AD/HD. And, a review of twin studies (Barkley 1998) suggests that up to 80% of the variance in the AD/HD trait of hyperactivity/impulsivity is genetic. This is an exciting area of interest that will surely reveal more over the next few years.

Brain Physiology

The most common symptoms associated with AD/HD implicate the frontal lobes and/or prefrontal cortex. The symptoms are lack of impulse control and critical learning from experience, as well as disorganization, poor self-monitoring, and weak social skills. Recently, scientists found that the frontal lobes and basal ganglia of AD/HD patients were about 10% smaller than a matched control group, (Castellanos 2001) and imaging studies reveal less brain activity in these areas as well. A new study (Castellanos, et al. 2002) reports that both girls and boys with AD/HD have a smaller *total* brain volume than those without the condition.

Frontal-Lobe Symmetry

Other AD/HD research has implicated over-symmetry between the left and right frontal lobes in the brain. In general, the left frontal lobe is more involved with approach behaviors and the right frontal lobe with avoidance behaviors. In normal subjects, the right frontal lobe is a bit larger than the left, which would seem to indicate a stronger tendency towards avoiding negative repercussions (or stronger impulse control).

Blood Flow

Some AD/HD research has implicated under-arousal of the central nervous system, particularly in the frontal lobes. As evidenced by PET scans, normalization occurs when the subjects are given stimulants to increase blood flow.

Neurotransmitter Dysfunction

Some AD/HD research has implicated the neurotransmitter dopamine. Dopamine pathways in the brain, which link the basal ganglia and prefrontal cortex (PFC), appear to play a major role in AD/HD. Insufficient "fuel"or stimulation in the PFC prevents this part of the brain from playing its standard impulse-regulation role. Stimulants typically reduce the flow of dopamine to this area. Serotonin involvement is also possible.

Traumatic Head Injury

Although the skull is bone, the brain is soft and upon impact can be launched into its hard casing, making it very susceptible to damage. The typical growing-up experience presents countless possibilities for injury: a fall from a bike, bunk bed, tree, or roof; a car accident, sports injury, fight, or physical abuse. Every one of these incidents puts a child at risk for subsequent learning and conduct problems. Why? The area that regulates impulse control, the prefrontal cortex, is the area of the brain most easily damaged.

Other Potential Risk Factors

Additional risk factors include a family history of alcoholism, female relatives that have Briquette's syndrome (hysteria/imagined illness), living in poverty, severe family relationship problems (e.g., a nasty divorce, abuse or neglect), retardation, conduct disorder, childhood lead poisoning, maternal smoking or drug use during pregnancy, and low birth weight.

AD/HD Risk Factors

Physiological

Prenatal

Environmental

- Premature birth
- Missing/damaged genes
- Exposure to drugs, toxins, nicotine, alcohol

- Reduced frontal-lobe blood flow
- Abnormal brain structures
- Attentional or motor area dysfunction
- Faulty neuron connectivity
- Chemical dysregulation
- Acquired brain insults

- Exposure to toxins
- Overexposure to infections/viruses
- Lack of infant attunement
- Insufficient motor or verbal exposure
- Acquired brain insults
- Exposure to trauma

Accommodation Tips

✎ Encourage peer interaction and cooperative activities; provide strategic support and leadership as the child learns to get along with others.

✎ Reduce potential distractions, such as environmental noise, windows, and doors; seat learners in a quiet area, near a good role model or by the teacher's desk.

✎ Hold regular family meetings to discuss behavioral issues and concerns in a relaxed, objective setting. Encourage input from all family members.

4

How to Get an Accurate Diagnosis

Because many children exhibit occasional inappropriate or hyperactive behaviors, widespread confusion exists about the diagnosis and treatment of AD/HD. Children who appear inattentive, hyperactive, or impulsive may be responding to a stressful family situation, classroom boredom, or a developmental stage that is normal. It is also critical to keep in mind that AD/HD symptoms are also characteristic of immature frontal lobes. As the frontal lobes mature (ages 12-25) we sometimes see a decline in these behaviors. This helps explain why experts suggest that an AD/HD diagnosis is more reliable in older children (more mature frontal lobes) and why an expert evaluation is necessary.

Common AD/HD Symptoms

- Poor mental calculation skills and highly variable skill performance
- Poor planning for future events; weak preparation skills
- Insensitivity to errors
- Calls out answers in class; rarely waits turn
- Frequently distracted and rarely finishes work
- Impaired sense of time passage
- No patience; wants everything right now
- Messy desk or personal space
- Inability to reflect on the past and learn from it
- Highly kinetic; always moving or fidgeting
- Limited short-term memory
- Lack of foresight or hindsight
- Sleep problems
- Messy writing
- Angry outbursts or crying fits

Recent studies (Gruber, et al. 2000; Stein 1999) indicate that AD/HD children show a very predictable instability in their sleep patterns, including irregularities in sleep onset, sleep duration, and amount of true sleep received. In fact, sleep pattern may contribute to a definitive diagnostic tool in the future, say researchers at the National Institute of Mental Health (2002). Because sleep is a critical time for encoding new learning, sleep problems reduce the likelihood of remembering complex learning (Peigneux, et al. 2001).

AD/HD signs may also include high sensitivity to noise levels and an overabundance of visual stimuli. Overstimulation may lead to excessive crying that ceases when a calm environment is established. It is not unusual for the AD/HD learner to get a glassy-eyed or comatose look during such episodes. Talking in streams or "chattering" is also common in AD/HD learners. When necessary redirect them towards a favored outlet (e.g., art, music, tactile stimulation, movement activity), rather than asking them to "stop talking."

The Diagnosis Controversy

Diagnosing AD/HD can be difficult because often the behavior-based symptoms of the condition only occur when attempting specific tasks and usually under specific environmental conditions. A second complication is that AD/HD is highly comorbid (overlaps with other disorders) 50-75% of the time (Semrud-Clikeman, et al. 1992). And a third reason is that although scientists are making progress in the effort to develop a reliable lab instrument for *confirming* the diagnosis of AD/HD, one has yet to be found (Dougherty, et al. 1999). Although blood work, urine analysis, chromosome studies, EEG's, average evoked responses and brain-imaging workups (e.g., MRIs and CT scans) provide valuable information, none of these tests alone are accurate in diagnosing AD/HD. Rather physicians must rely on a series of evaluative, observational measures, while ruling out "look-alike" conditions and external factors to correctly diagnose the condition. A substantial amount of time is necessary for a comprehensive examination; thus, most primary-care physicians refer patients suspected of having AD/HD to specialists who can devote the time and repeat appointments necessary for a thorough diagnosis and follow up.

Diagnosing AD/HD can be difficult because often the behavior-based symptoms of the condition only occur when attempting specific tasks and usually under specific environmental conditions.

Beyond the time challenges of diagnosing AD/HD and the requirement that educators refer children through the appropriate protocol, many believe we overmedicate children in an effort to control "undesirable" behaviors that may, in fact, be appropriate for their mental, emotional, and physical development. While the production of methylphenidate (sold as Ritalin or Concerta) and amphetamines (Dexedrine, Adderall) soared between 1993 and 1999 (see graph below), many researchers, physicians, and educators insist that this increase is justifiable based on the growing awareness and treatment options now available. Others, however, contend that the makers of Ritalin deliberately and negligently promoted the diagnosis of AD/HD and sales of Ritalin, while failing to appropriately address the hazards of the drug's use (Breggin 2001). The trend, however, towards prescribing medication before exhausting the alternatives seems to be leveling off.

Growth in Production of Common AD/HD Drugs

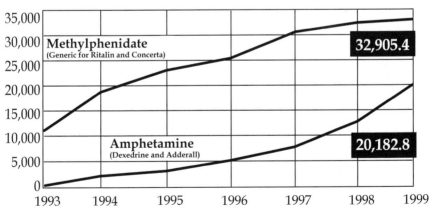

Source: US Drug Enforcement Administration

Prescriptions filled in the USA to treat AD/HD have begun to level off, but prior to 1999 production of AD/HD medications soared.

Finally, the diagnosis and treatment controversy is complicated by the fact that children with mild to moderate AD/HD symptoms are usually able to maintain a modicum of control in flexible environments. Therefore, it is important to determine to *what degree* a learner is impacted by the condition and in *which environments,* before creating a treatment plan. if a child does not have severe symptoms, accommodate rather than medicate.

A Constellation of AD/HD Responses
Depending on Severity

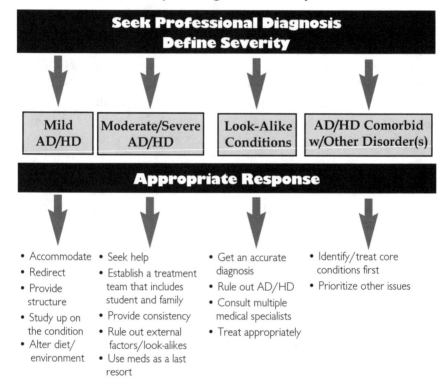

Seek Professional Diagnosis
Define Severity

Mild AD/HD	Moderate/Severe AD/HD	Look-Alike Conditions	AD/HD Comorbid w/Other Disorder(s)

Appropriate Response

- Accommodate
- Redirect
- Provide structure
- Study up on the condition
- Alter diet/environment

- Seek help
- Establish a treatment team that includes student and family
- Provide consistency
- Rule out external factors/look-alikes
- Use meds as a last resort

- Get an accurate diagnosis
- Rule out AD/HD
- Consult multiple medical specialists
- Treat appropriately

- Identify/treat core conditions first
- Prioritize other issues

Students with serious AD/HD symptoms who are still experiencing problems at school despite accommodations, ought to be referred to a pediatric specialist. A comprehensive diagnosis will usually include:

- ☞ A complete family history, including medical, psychological, academic, and emotional/social functioning
- ☞ Interviews with significant others and teachers
- ☞ Observation in natural settings, not just in the doctor's office
- ☞ Intelligence testing (sometimes included)

- Observation over time to understand the depth/scope of the condition
- Use of a rating scale to capture the degree of impairment
- Assessment of developmental abilities, attention span, and impulsivity
- Thorough and regular follow-up examinations

If a student with moderate to severe AD/HD is *not* appropriately diagnosed and treated, they run a serious risk of failure. They also are more likely to develop overlapping behavioral disturbances and personality disorders. The seriousness of this condition when left untreated or ignored warrants vigilance in referring students suspected of having AD/HD to the appropriate professionals in a timely manner.

An AD/HD diagnosis is usually based on the sum of teachers' and parents' reports about how a child behaves in different settings. These reports are especially important keys to diagnosing AD/HD because a child may not exhibit symptoms in the doctor's office. He/she may be able to "behave" and "pay attention" for a short period of time or when communicating on a one-to-one basis. Besides examining the child for AD/HD, the physician is also ruling out look-alike conditions and the possibility of comorbidities (or overlapping conditions).

Since students with AD/HD frequently have comorbid conditions (i.e., conduct disorder, oppositional-defiant disorder, depressive disorder), diagnosis can be tricky. In fact,

> *AD/HD is diagnosed in 7% - 17% of children in the United States and accounts for half of all visits to child psychiatric clinics.*
> —Barbaresi, et al. 2002

as many as 50% of AD/HD sufferers, develop conduct disorders and about 25% also have learning disabilities. Vision, hearing, and developmental problems also need to be ruled out before making an AD/HD diagnosis.

What Brain Scans Reveal

Parents sometimes request a brain scan to support an AD/HD diagnosis. Both PET and SPECT scans can show the areas of the brain that are metabolically under-active or over-active (see SPECT scans on the following page). Such tests, however, are expensive ($1200-$2500 each), are not widely used yet for diagnostic purposes, and are rarely covered by health insurance. In the near future, brain-imaging studies may be relied upon more to confirm an AD/HD diagnosis. Scientists are making progress with a new imaging agent called Altropane, which is under current review by the Food and Drug Administration (Dougherty, et al. 1999).

SPECT Scans Reveal Differences Between Normal and AD/HD Brain During Concentration

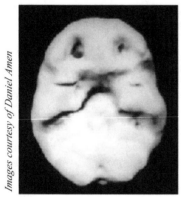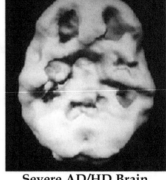

Images courtesy of Daniel Amen

Normal Brain   **Severe AD/HD Brain**

Normally, the brain should be more active in concentration states. Lighter areas in the normal brain on the left reflect greater metabolic activity. Darker areas in the AD/HD brain on the right suggest underactivity.

Brain scans, thus, provide concrete physical evidence of the differences. If the diagnosis is positive, and AD/HD is confirmed, do not ignore it. There are a number of good options available for treating the condition. Ironically, students with AD/HD can be very smart. Teaching them the basic skills alone is not enough. They need to be taught with a gentle approach *how* to recognize and appropriately manage their impulses. Traditional approaches to discipline, such as punishment for not listening, distracting others, or forgetting homework, are not recommended for the AD/HD learner. Rather, set reasonable limits on issues of importance and provide more structure, feedback, and accommodation.

Why More Boys Are Being Diagnosed

The gender issue regarding AD/HD is a complex one. Although the condition is generally diagnosed in boys more than girls, a new study suggests that the reason for this disparity is that girls generally exhibit the inattentive subtype, which is harder to diagnose (Biederman, et al. 2002). In contrast, another new study reports that the numbers of girls and boys being diagnosed with AD/HD today is nearly equal (Robison, et al. 2002). Girls with AD/HD are more likely than boys to have lower IQ and achievement scores (Rucklidge & Tannock 2001), but are less likely to have a learning disability or problems at school (Biederman, et al. 2002). Another illuminating study (Zakon 1977) suggests that the effect of estrogen in girls may mitigate AD/HD symptoms. This could explain why females with AD/HD have greater metabolic disturbances and cognitive deficits than males early on, but their difficulties don't show up until adolescence (Ernst, et al. 1998).

Look-Alike Conditions: How Not to Get Fooled!

Many common conditions mimic AD/HD. They include auditory-processing deficits, sensory-integration disorders, stress disorders, oppositional-defiant disorder, allergies, depression, and developmental disorders. Some of the most common look-alike conditions are:

Auditory-Processing Deficits

Students with an auditory-processing deficit will commonly have trouble with following directions and reading and will be easily distracted due to problems processing sounds.

Sensory-Integration Disorders

Students with a sensory-integration disorder usually have difficulty paying attention or focusing due to problems processing incoming sensory data. They often take unreasonable risks and are poorly organized.

Stress Disorders

Affected students often show trance-like states, have difficulty concentrating, and exhibit short-term memory deficits due to a dysregulated stress response.

Oppositional-Defiant Disorder

This chronic and serious behavioral disorder is often comorbid with AD/HD and is characterized by verbal aggressiveness, difficulty following directions, rarely learning from the past, difficulty planning for the future, and chronic lack of sociability.

Allergies and Toxins

Allergic or toxic reactions correlate with poor concentration, inability to focus and listen, difficulty following directions, and memory problems. Toxins in the environment, such as lead (found in dust, soil, and flaking paint in areas where leaded paint and gasoline were once used) may disrupt brain processes which mimic the symptoms of AD/HD. However, a simple blood test can rule out lead poisoning.

Learning Disorders

Learning disorders include reading disorder, mathematics disorder, disorder of written expression, and learning disorder not otherwise specified. Children with learning disorders are likely to exhibit memory problems; however, the memory deficits are not due to poor listening as in AD/HD. Rather the memory deficit is caused by the learning disorder.

Developmental Disorders

Developmental disorders include motor-skills disorder (i.e., immature Symmetric Tonic Neck Reflex or STNR), communication disorders (i.e., tics, stuttering), and pervasive developmental disorders (i.e., Asperger's). Some of these conditions share common symptoms, such as inattention, impulsivity, and hyperactivity; however, children with specific learning or developmental disorders are more likely to exhibit difficulties in multiple contexts (at home, play, and/or in other social settings). Children with AD/HD, usually exhibit problem behaviors only at school or in constricting environments.

Overlapping/Comorbid Conditions

An added difficulty in diagnosing AD/HD is that it often coexists with other medical problems. In fact, a minority of sufferers have AD/HD alone over the course of their lifetime. Conversely, 56% of sufferers have four or more psychiatric comorbidities throughout their lifetime. About 11% of sufferers experience one other psychiatric condition, and 18% have three.

While AD/HD does not *cause* conduct disorder, bipolar disorder, or violent behavior, it is *correlated* with negative conduct. In fact, as many as one-third of children diagnosed with AD/HD, are not only hyperactive and impulsive but also aggressors who break rules and hurt others, according to *The Harvard Mahoney Neuroscience Institute Letter* (2001). Researchers speculate that these misbehaviors may have the same root in the brain; all of them reflect a lack of impulse control (ibid). The crux of the problem is that AD/HD patients are often given medications without the social interventions to support positive behavioral change. Students who "act out" are typically perceived and treated negatively by adults; this impacts their environment, and ultimately changes everyone's response in "the loop."

This viscous cycle can feed the student's feelings of anger, inadequacy, and abnormality, thereby increasing the risk of substance abuse and other negatively correlated factors. A disconcerting statistic reveals that as many as 65% of children with AD/HD will develop dysfunctional social behaviors often leading to alcohol and drug abuse and trouble with the law. These children can be stubborn, have outbursts of temper, and act belligerently or defiantly. At times, these behaviors may progress into more serious conduct disorders. Children with this combination of problems may fall into trouble with school officials, take unsafe risks, or break laws by stealing, setting fires, destroying property, or driving recklessly. One study (Sachs, et al. 2000) reports that people with bi-polar disorder (manic- depression) have an earlier onset of symptoms if they also have AD/HD.

Many children with AD/HD also have a specific learning disability, which means that they have trouble mastering language or certain skills such as reading, math, or handwriting. Although AD/HD is not categorized as a *learning* disorder, its interference with concentration and attention make it sometimes even *more difficult* for a child to perform well in school. Some with AD/HD also have memory problems that need separate assessment and treatment. "The memory deficits are caused by a learning disability and affect short-term memory skills used for spelling, sounding out words, and other reading-related tasks," reports Lynn Richman, Ph.D., professor of pediatric psychology at University of Iowa. Memory testing can help reveal whether a child has trouble learning because of poor listening skills, usually caused by AD/HD, or because of difficulty remembering things, usually caused by a learning disability.

This may explain why children with AD/HD who receive medication for their condition oftentimes still show memory problems. "Medication can improve attention in children with AD/HD may not solve the learning problems related to memory," Richman reports. "We need to find out if other medications can treat AD/HD while also addressing memory deficits, and help children get specialized memory training and other educational interventions in addition to their AD/HD treatment."

Appropriate Age for Confirming An AD/HD Diagnosis

To fully understand and accurately identify AD/HD, it is necessary to consider the age of the sufferer. Although it is not uncommon for preschoolers to be diagnosed, many experts believe this is too early for an accurate diagnosis. In four- and five-year-olds, both inattention and hyperactivity are common; however, by age six or seven, children who have trouble controlling their impulses may be exhibiting a symptom of AD/HD. At ten, students with AD/HD may know *what* to do, but not *where* to do it. This challenge reflects the differences in "brain systems" at work and is one of the core reasons why an accurate diagnosis is controversial by nature. Since the condition is contextual or situational, it may be apparent in one setting, yet not another. For example, it may be obvious at school during silent reading, but not while meeting with the doctor one on one.

Although AD/HD medications should rarely be administered in or before kindergarten, some early signs of the condition may be apparent at this age. In a recent Dalhousie University study (DeWolfe, et al. 2000), researchers observed 50 three- to six-year-olds in a preschool setting, half diagnosed with AD/HD and half not. The AD/HD preschoolers were off-task significantly more time than the non-AD/HD children and were more talkative and active. From this, the researchers concluded that early identification of AD/HD may be valid and useful in establishing behavioral interventions at an early age; however, the suspected diagnosis cannot be confirmed until later and medication is rarely considered appropriate at this age.

Although, AD/HD represents a serious challenge, the condition itself is treatable. Many children with AD/HD lead very

Children with AD/HD are often given medications without the social interventions to support positive behavioral change.

successful lives. When left untreated, however, the condition is more likely to worsen and be complicated with comorbid or overlapping conditions, such as depression, mood disorders, and conduct disorders. The first step, therefore, is an early and accurate diagnosis. Don't be afraid to get the professional opinion of multiple specialists if necessary.

A Better Diagnostic Instrument

For the first time, brain scans have revealed measurable biochemical differences in people with AD/HD, a discovery that could reduce the number of children mistakenly diagnosed and put on drug treatment, (Dougherty, et al. 1999). "This is the most promising development I've seen in a long time in terms of our coming up with an actual physical test that could help pin down the diagnosis of AD/HD," reports Dr. Edward Hallowell, a Boston psychiatrist and AD/HD expert.

Using a radioactively tagged chemical agent called Altropane that attaches to dopamine transporters when ingested by the patient, researchers can measure the subject's dopamine balance, which is thought to impact movement, thought, motivation, and pleasure. Doctors will still have to evaluate a child's behavior to diagnose the disease, but the new test could be an important diagnostic tool, the researchers report.

Highly Effective Treatments

Depending on the severity of a child's AD/HD and his/her reactions to initial accommodations, a constellation of responses is appropriate. The following diagram depicts the possibilities and appropriate responses. Physicians generally only recommend drug therapy after non-drug alternatives have been exhausted and rarely before age 6.

ACCOMMODATE

➥ You can make accommodations that, not only respect and assist the AD/HD learner, but make it possible for him/her to succeed in class.
GOOD CHOICE

TREAT

➥ You can take a team approach involving the student, parents, and school personnel that provides specific long-term interventions and support. Treatment can make a difference between a students' eventual success or failure.
GOOD CHOICE, IF APPLICABLE TO ROLE

IGNORE

➥ You can ignore the condition, hoping it will go away or that the student will succeed despite it.
BAD CHOICE

Essential First Steps:
Accommodate, Accommodate, Accommodate

Remember, it is often easier to change the learner by adapting the environment to his/her specific needs (thus changing his/her response) than to force changes on the student that are rooted in their biology and not *truly* supported by the environment. Non-drug treatments include classroom accommodations, redirection, diet changes, biofeedback, a reward system for appropriate behaviors/performance, and training/therapy for teachers and parents to improve contingency-management skills.

Federal disability laws mandate educational accommodations be available for children with AD/HD, and modifications in public-school settings can be as important to your child's treatment as medical intervention. Special parenting skills are often needed because children with AD/HD are not as responsive to common parenting practices—especially punishment as the lone practice. Cognitive behavioral therapy can help a child monitor his/her own behavior and introduce effective problem-solving strategies. AD/HD children also have a special need for good relationships with children their own age, so having friends is a big help.

Accommodation Tips

- ☞ Create a structured, predictable environment. Provide consistent seating arrangements, a daily schedule, rules, expectations, and consequences.

- ☞ Create social behavior goals with learners and implement an immediate reward system (e.g., involving them in presentations, providing praise, special responsibilities, or time in favored activities).

- ☞ Provide frequent feedback and contact. This will help keep the AD/HD learner on task.

- ☞ Monitor closely during transitions, excursions, and schedule changes.

- ☞ Break up tasks into workable and obtainable steps so student can see an end to the work.

Mild to Moderate AD/HD Symptoms

Students with *mild* AD/HD will
exhibit frequent frustration and
annoyance, but often "figure out"
that they are a bit different and
learn to make accommodations.
With a few good, caring teachers
on their side, children with mild
AD/HD are likely to be successful in life. A mentor who shares a

common passion or hobby can make a lifelong difference in the AD/HD
child's life. As the student experiences incremental success in something
and begins to feel competent in even just one subject area or skill set,
he/she takes one giant step towards succeeding in school. Sometimes
this path is forged despite an unawareness of the child's condition, but
other times, kids with mild AD/HD, unfortunately, fall through the
cracks and get left behind.

Accommodation Tips

☞ Provide advance warning when a transition is going to
   occur (e.g., "Now we are completing the worksheet; next
   we will get out our homework to review.")

☞ Provide learners with a definite purpose during unstruc-
   tured activities (e.g., "The purpose of going to the library is
   to check out a book that will help you with your report.")

Severe AD/HD Symptoms

Students with more severe symptoms generally have trouble in school
and are at higher risk for academic failure and other problems. However,
these learners aren't as likely to fall through the cracks as children with
mild AD/HD. If they are recognized and provided the appropriate behavioral and medical interventions, they can do very well in school.

However, they will need *both* accommodation and a highly structured program of learning based on a consistent routine that empowers rather than disempowers by reinforcing dependency or helplessness. In helping children with severe AD/HD symptoms, parents, teachers and physicians need to work together to devise a practical plan of behavioral treatments at school and home.

Teaching behavior modification can have remarkable results. It's not the instant gratification you get with a pill, but the results do come. I've seen those remarkable changes first-hand in my own son. When he was in kindergarten unable to sit, pay attention, or focus on the teacher, she suggested we put him on Ritalin. Instead, I found a doctor willing to treat the child, not the symptoms. We cleaned up his diet, taught him how to recognize when his mind was wandering and how to bring it back. We worked with his teachers to develop a learning program: Verbal instructions are repeated to him one-on-one; long-term reading assignments and projects are broken down into small segments, and important tests are taken in a quiet spot away from classmates and distractions. Today he is doing well in high school, thanks in no small part to the help and understanding of his teachers. He tells me that it's still a struggle some days to focus, but he feels proud that he's been able to learn how to control his attention without the aid of drugs.

—LeAnna Washington
Dem. State Rep.

Diet/Nutritional Supplements

Altering one's diet is far more effective for those with mild versus severe AD/HD symptoms. Nutritional supplements containing naturally occurring (not refined) sugar derivatives or complex carbohydrates (i.e., rice, pasta, popcorn and potatoes) versus simple carbs (i.e., potato chips, candy bars, and refined flour products) can decrease the number and severity of symptoms associated with AD/HD, researchers report (Dykman & Dykman 1998).

For reasons still unknown, glyco-nutritional supplements given to 17 AD/HD children in a six-week study significantly improved the subjects' ability to focus their hyperactivity and attention. Given in capsule form, the supplements contained such sugar derivatives as glucose, mannose, and galactose—nutrients known to be important to normal physical and cognitive function. Although further research is needed to draw specific conclusions, children with AD/HD are often found deficient in certain vitamins, sugars, minerals, and essential fatty acids (Colquhoun 1994).

In general, a high-protein/low-carbohydrate diet supports AD/HD sufferers since excess carbohydrates can negatively impact dopamine levels. The high protein/low-carbohydrate combination also helps stabilize blood-sugar levels. Tyrosine and Gingko Biloba supplements can help increase blood flow and activity in the frontal lobe—the brain area most implicated in AD/HD. Tyrosine, a neurotransmitter, is eventually converted to dopamine which supports AD/HD function as well. Tyrosine tablets (children - 250mg 2 times/day; adults - 1000mg 2 times/day) may be more effective when AD/HD symptoms are mild. It's also a good idea to support your child's healthy diet of whole foods with a high quality multi-vitamin/mineral supplement taken first thing in the morning on an empty stomach. In addition, grape-seed extract has been found to be helpful in some case studies; however, a large-scale study has yet to be conducted.

While it is true that there are clear links between dietary consumption and behaviors, pinpointing particular reactions will probably require the assistance of a professional nutritionist. There are many potential food allergies that can exacerbate the problem. Some parents claim that a diet high in protein and *complex* carbohydrates (i.e., potatoes, pasta, and rice) with plenty of fruits and vegetables versus lots of *simple* carbohydrates (i.e., chips, cookies, and sugar cereals) benefits their

AD/HD child. A dietary solution such as this, although appealing, has yet to be *proven* effective in large-scale, double blind, peer-reviewed clinical trials. This is not to say, however, that it doesn't help.

NeuroFeedback

Some sufferers are helped by alternative therapeutic approaches, such as biofeedback, also called NeuroFeedback. This is a treatment activity that uses simple EEG instruments to measure bodily reactions (like pulse rate, breathing, or sweating) while the AD/HD learner performs certain tasks. The information fed back to the learner helps them become more aware of their physical responses while helping to affect change. For example, if the learner is trying to match up items on a computer screen, they can see how their anxiety level increases the harder they try. With practice, they can learn to consciously slow down their breathing and heart rate to facilitate better concentration and learning. While the effectiveness of biofeedback has been shown in some studies, the treatment remains unfairly controversial because of the so-called "mind-control" aspect of the process (it's your own mind you're learning to control). Yet, when facilitated by a skilled professional, some learners have experienced success at retraining their frontal lobes, thereby, decreasing impulsivity and increasing concentration. One online resource for more information on NeuroFeedback is www.futurehealth.org/brainmas.htm

Like biofeedback, NeuroFeedback is a non-drug therapy whereby patients are taught to control specific brainwave patterns by becoming more sensitized to their body responses and mind patterns. This is an interesting development because some studies have shown that EEG brain abnormalities are present in persons with AD/HD (Monastra, et al. 2001), specifically Beta- and Theta-wave activity (Barry, et al. 2002). The good new is you don't have to worry about side effects when using non-drug alternatives such as NeuroFeedback. Some claim this treatment is the most promising alternative to drug therapy to date (Brue & Oakland 2002).

Drug Therapy

Standard pharmaceutical treatment for AD/HD includes psychostimulants, such as Ritalin/Concerta (methylphenidate) and Adderall or Dexedrine (amphetamine), which have been shown to increase compliance, improve academic performance, and lower hyperactivity

(Goldman, et al. 1998). Although stimulant drug therapy for the treatment of children with AD/HD is controversial, doctors have prescribed methylphenidate for over 50 years without confirmed long-term side effects. Medications can result in an improvement in core symptoms, such as impulsive behavior and inattention, but therapeutic support may be necessary to help the child establish positive and effective work and social habits. Since AD/HD medications are most effective when used in conjunction with behavioral therapy, if the child is over six years of age and has severe AD/HD symptoms, both treatments are likely to be part of the child's IEP (Individual Education Plan).

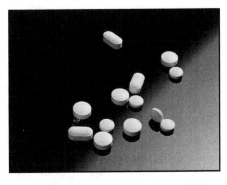

According to the *Physicians Desk Reference*, a standard resource used by the medical community, more than 10% of AD/HD patients who are prescribed methylphenidate experience short-term side effects such as delay in going to sleep, insomnia, reduced appetite, weight loss, tics, agitation, irritability, jitteriness, stomachaches, and headaches. These side effects are usually short-lived and can be mitigated by adjusting the dose and timing of medication. Some patients find improvement with the physician-recommended dose, while others find *a milder dose* is effective and may reduce side effects. This is why it is important to pay close attention to physical or bio-rhythmic changes while identifying the best dose for each individual.

> **With the most severe core behaviors of AD/HD, psychological therapies without medications do not appear to be optimally effective. Children who regularly take their medication _and_ practice behavior techniques routinely do better than those who rely on one or the other.**
>
> —American Medical Association
> www.ama.org

Stimulant medications are available in short, intermediate, and recently, in long-acting formulas. One product currently under investigation is a transdermal patch that can be applied once daily to administer methylphenidate so that children don't have to take a pill at school. Concerta (methylphenidate) also comes in a slow-release pill that is taken in the morning before the child leaves for school. Alternatives to stimulant drugs include antidepressants and anti-convulsants. Also, a new non-stimulant drug, Atomoxetine, has recently become available.

Methylphenidate works by increasing catecholimines at the synapse in the same way that Selective Serotonin Reuptake Inhibitors do in the treatment of depression. By blocking the reuptake (or exit) of key neurotransmitters, the target chemical lingers longer and its effect is intensified. Methylphenidate blocks the reuptake of dopamine, the feel-good chemical that provides a reward effect, while also blocking the reuptake of noradrenaline, known as our get-up-and-go or action neuro-transmitter. Both dopamine and noradrenaline are thought to work by charging up the frontal lobes, giving them the fuel necessary to regulate impulses, time, and working memory.

Because no single AD/HD medication always works for every child, doctors depend on the input of teachers and parents in the initial stages of drug therapy. Sometimes more than one drug must be tried before a child's behavior improves and any side effects are mitigated. No matter what medication is prescribed, even successful treatment needs to be re-evaluated each year, especially if there is any reason to suspect that the medicine is no longer needed or the dosage can be reduced.

> *In helping a child with severe AD/HD, parents, teachers, and doctors need to work together. This requires substantial time, commitment, and coordination, and usually depends on a combination of medication and a practical plan of behavioral treatments to be implemented at both home and school.*

How AD/HD Drugs Impact the Impulsive Brain

Methylphenidate (Ritalin/Concerta), the most common AD/HD medication, belongs to a class of drugs called Central Nervous System (CNS) stimulants. Due to fewer side effects, methylphenidate is regarded as the first-line medication if non-drug alternatives fail. The drug is formulated as a tablet and is also available in a sustained-release (or long-acting) form. The sustained-release capsule is usually taken once per day before breakfast.

In general, 75% to 80% of children with AD/HD will show some improvement on stimulants (if not one, then another), particularly if the proper dosage, such as up to 1 mg per kg of body weight per day, is used (Goldman, et al. 1998; NIH 2002). A study at the University of Pittsburgh, School of Medicine looked at highly aggressive children diagnosed with AD/HD. Half the children were given a placebo (sugar pill) and the other half were administered methylphenidate (Ritalin/Concerta). In the double-blind study, the methylphenidate group showed a significant reduction in aggressive behavior.

Methylphenidate works by interfering with dopamine (a common neurotransmitter, often known as the "brain's reward chemical"). Sensitivity to the action of methylphenidate may vary depending on the genetic etiology of the dopaminergic dysfunction. Some patients find that medication helps them control unwanted behaviors long enough to achieve substantial success with behavioral interventions. For 20% to 30% of patients treated with medications, however, the treatment fails. Failure is usually associated with intolerable side effects, inappropriate treatment, misdiagnoses, or complexities caused by a comorbid condition.

It has been suggested that the long-term use of stimulants or amphetamines prescribed for children may lead to substance-use disorder. However, a recent study (Biederman, et al. 2000-b) found that *untreated AD/HD* represented *more* of a risk factor for substance-use disorder in adolescent subjects than those treated early with psychostimulants. In fact, *treated* AD/HD was associated with a significant 85% *risk reduction* for substance-use disorder relative to untreated AD/HD (ibid). In short, pharmaceutical treatment for AD/HD may actually *help prevent* drug abuse in AD/HD patients by eliminating the desire for illicit drug consumption as a form of self-medication.

Methylphenidate can be habit-form-ing. Do not take a higher dose than prescribed, or take it more often, or for longer periods than your doctor recommends.

—The National Institute of Health
www.nlm.nih.gov/

However, others argue that medication creates a mentality of dependency; that children are getting the message they don't need to adapt, grow, or change, but simply take a pill. And then there's the question of whether taking medication may reduce the subject's sense of control and self-efficacy. This issue represents the heart of the controversy surrounding the "ritalin craze."

Although medications can result in an improvement in core symptoms such as impulsive behavior and inattention as well as improved school and social performances, studies have found that psychostimulants, such as methylphenidate (Ritalin/Concerta), dextroamphetamine (Dexedrine), amphetamine (Adderall) are most effective when combined with behavior therapy (NIH 2002). Sometimes antidepressants are also used. They are thought to work by modulating the neurotransmitters (substances that send nerve impulses), such as dopamine, noradrenaline, and serotonin in the brain. This has led to further investigation into the role of each of these neurotransmitters in AD/HD. Volkow and colleagues (2001) speculate that by increasing the levels of extracellular dopamine, motivational circuits are activated, which in turn make the tasks children perform seem more stimulating and compelling.

There appears to be an optimal window of learning opportunity after administering AD/HD medication. In a recent study involving 9- to 11-year-old boys, reading was greatly improved (mastery, fewer errors, higher rate per minute) during the first hour after taking a dose of methylphenidate compared to 3 to 4 hours after medication (Kastner, et al. 2000).

Accommodation Tips

- Teach and emphasize key words; distribute handouts with important notes underlined.

- Show learners how to plan a project, outline a paper, and brainstorm ideas; assist student in setting short-term goals.

- Provide extra time for AD/HD learners to complete assignments and testing. Teach test-taking skills and strategies and use clear, uncluttered forms. For tests that require writing, provide lines with ample answer space.

- Create a behavior contract; ignore minor, inappropriate behaviors, but use time-out protocol for a consequence to serious misbehavior.

Is There a Dark Side to AD/HD Medications?

The most frequent side effects associated with AD/HD medications are reduced appetite (21% - meds vs. 3% - placebo) and delayed sleep onset (75% - meds vs. 5% - placebo) (Castellanos & Tannock 2001). Although these short-term side effects can be eliminated with discontinuance or mitigated by adjusting dose and timing of the medication, some concerns about long-term consequences for use in children (especially prior to age 6) have been raised. Therefore, the decision to give children psychostimulants should never be taken lightly. Although it is not the norm, drug-induced obsessive-compulsive reactions, growth suppression, and potential changes in brain function and structure similar to those that occur with amphetamine and cocaine use are possible long-term consequences of early drug therapy in children (Breggin 2001).

Since the growing brain is a fragile organ, AD/HD drugs should only be used as a last resort in children, and rarely in children under the age of six. Additionally, methylphenidate should *not* be used in patients with severe depression or with psychosis since it can exacerbate the symptoms of psychological disturbance and thought disorder.

I'm not trying to attack the psychiatrists who prescribe stimulants or the companies that make it. But with the pitfalls, parents need to explore all treatment options, especially the drug-free ones, before giving their children this powerful and sometimes dangerous pill. The U.S. Drug Enforcement Agency has labeled Ritalin a class one narcotic, sharing that spotlight with morphine, opium, and cocaine.

—Bruce Wiseman
Citizens Commission on Human Rights

Potential Adverse Drug Reactions

Although methylphenidate has been prescribed for more than 50 years in the treatment of AD/HD, some assert it has negative implications for children over the long run. One effect, for example, that has been reported (Funk, et al 1993) is a loss of creativity. An AD/HD prescription may make a child more manageable in the classroom, but at what cost? This is a question that many parents (and educators) are grappling with today.

One long-term study suggests that 10% of patients report serious adverse reactions to methylphenidate (Cherland & Fitzpatrick 1999). With regard to the problem of drug-induced obsessive-compulsive reactions alone, a National Institute of Health Web site lists three pages of cautions regarding methylphenidate (NIH 2002). Additionally, children on psychostimulants are sometimes mistakenly diagnosed with a psychiatric disorder and subjected to additional medications or they are given antidepressants, antianxiety medications, sedatives, and even neuroleptics (lately Risperidone) to facilitate withdrawal from psychostimulants.

Possible Brain Changes

Animal studies conducted by biophysics professor Joan Baizer and colleagues at the University of New York at Buffalo (Castellanos & Tannock 2001) suggest that methylphenidate may initiate changes in brain function and structure similar to those that occur with illicit amphetamine and cocaine use. In particular, the research implicates C-FOS genes, which are associated with nerve-cell function in the striatum—a brain structure important to movement, motivation, and addiction (ibid). Other critics of Ritalin, including physician Peter Breggin (2001), assert that AD/HD medications can cause permanent, irreversible brain damage in the form of biochemical dysfunction, neurotransmitter receptor loss, and brain-cell death, but the data to support this assertion has not been substantiated.

Growth Suppression

Some reports (Funk, et al. 1993) suggest that methylphenidate use in children can result in growth suppression (i.e., in weight and/or height)—an effect commonly linked with appetite suppressants. Although most children make up for any growth stunts once off the medication, hormone disruption can impair the normal development of organs, including the brain. Since many children remain on methylphenidate throughout the year and for many years at a time, it can't be assumed they will recover their growth during drug holidays. Furthermore, it must be emphasized that the accelerated growth during rebound is itself abnormal.

Potential Abuse

Lastly, parents and educators should be aware that non-prescribed Ritalin/Concerta use is one of the latest forms of drug abuse on school campuses. Chemically similar to cocaine, oral ingestion dilutes the drug, but injections by needle show cocaine-like addictive qualities (Volkow, et al. 1995). If a student is required to take their AD/HD medication while at school, they should always follow school or the district's protocol for handling such matters.

Growing Movement Against Drug Therapy for AD/HD Children

There is a growing national movement against prescribing drugs for children with AD/HD. The founder of the movement, Peter Breggin, is the Director of The International Center for the Study of Psychiatry and Psychology and is an outspoken critic of the "drug solution." He is the author of numerous books on the subject, including *Talking Back to Ritalin, Your Drug May Be Your Problem*, and *Reclaiming Our*

Children. While some people dismiss Dr. Breggin as an overzealous critic, he has filed a class-action lawsuit that charges Novartis (the manufacturer of Ritalin), ChADD (Children and Adults with Attention-Deficit Disorder), and the American Psychiatric Association of committing fraud in conspiring to over-promote the diagnosis of AD/HD and its treatment with the stimulant drug Ritalin.

The lawsuit charges that the drug company "deliberately, intentionally, and negligently promoted the diagnosis of AD/HD and sales of Ritalin through its promotional literature and through its training of sales representatives. In so doing, despite knowledge of such problems and/or adverse reactions, defendants willfully failed to address or provide adequate information to consumers, doctors, and/or schools concerning many significant hazards of methylphenidate...." Whether the suit is proven in a court of law or not remains to be seen.

A Non-Stimulant Medication Now Available

Popular stimulant medications, such as Ritalin/Concerta (methylphenidate), Adderall, and Dexedrine (amphetamine), commonly

used in the treatment of children with AD/HD have long been controversial due, in part, to potential abuse in the wrong hands. Now, scientists have developed a *non-stimulant* medication called Atomoxetine to treat AD/HD. It's the first medicine available to treat adults and the only non-stimulant drug available to treat children with AD/HD. "Atomoxetine reduces the AD/HD symptoms of inattention and impulsivity without relying on a Schedule II controlled substance—a finding physicians have been waiting for," reports Dr. Lenard Adler, Associate Professor of Clinical Psychiatry and Neurology at New York University School of Medicine. The medication works by blocking norepinephrine transporters, which allows the norepinephrine to remain in the cell longer.

6   *Solutions for Parents*

Clearly, having a child with AD/HD can be a frustrating experience. This is why it is so important to keep the big picture in mind. Be sure your child knows that they are loved and valued despite what they do or don't do. Does this mean we should overlook inappropriate behaviors? No. Rather, guide your child gently and patiently towards a clear goal with mini-milestones in between. In the process, make sure you instill in him/her the following:

1. **A sense that they have some control over their own lives.**
2. **A sense that *what* they do is different from *who* they are.**
3. **A feeling that they are loved despite their condition.**

Gather Information

If you suspect your child may have AD/HD, begin to gather information. Consider the following questions in determining whether to have him/her assessed by a physician, psychologist, or other health specialist:

1. **Are the troubling behaviors excessive and pervasive? Do they occur more often than peer norms?**
2. **Are the troubling behaviors chronic, not just a response to a temporary situation?**
3. **Do the troubling behaviors occur in several settings, not just at school or at home?**

If the answer to all of these questions is yes, a professional assessment is recommended. Depending on the severity of symptoms, AD/HD is largely managed with accommodations that create a more compatible environment for the AD/HD learner.

The following key strategies can help to ensure the AD/HD child's success:

Modify the Environment

Attend to your child's need for an uncluttered, calm environment or space to retreat to. Ask your child's teacher to place him/her close to the front of the classroom; limit open spaces, which may encourage hyperactive behaviors and reduce distracting stimuli.

Provide Clear Instructions

Keep oral instructions simple and brief and repeat them at least once or twice each time. For multi-step processes, provide written instructions (and review them orally); always break up tasks and homework into small steps. Politely request that the child repeat instructions back to you so you can check for understanding.

Focus on Success

Provide both formal and informal feedback (such as point charts and compliments) to reinforce your child's progress.

Role Model Organization Skills

Establish daily checklists; help your child start a homework notebook with due dates listed and textbooks/supplies needed; encourage her/him to check it daily to ensure due dates are met.

Encourage Computer Use

Encourage the use of a computer with older children (age 10+); de-emphasize spelling errors and neatness and rather focus on content; offer help with handwriting skills.

Teach Proofreading Skills

Urge your child to slow down when completing answers. Demonstrate how to recheck work before submitting it. When working with your child to proof an assignment, ask key questions rather than "correcting" the paper for them.

Emphasize Effective Communication

Teach your child how powerful his/her words can be. Encourage verbal versus physical expression of anger. Role model appropriate interpersonal relationship skills such as how to apologize, ask for clarification, problem solve, and be a good listener.

Build Self-Esteem

Encourage performance in your child's areas of strength; provide feedback privately; do not ask her/him to perform a task publicly that is too difficult; focus on positive reinforcement. Role model success skills such as perseverance, practice, and follow through.

Learn Behavior-Modification Skills

Target a few unacceptable behaviors with clear consistent consequences explained privately to your child; consequences should not be publicly humiliating. Use hand signals (e.g., finger up) and verbal cues (e.g., "John, please take a 'break'") to privately communicate inappropriate behavior. A key component for success with behavior modification is consistency over time. When using "time-outs" for a consequence, keep the focus on "taking a 'break'" to calm down or reorient rather than punish.

Use Active-Learning Techniques

Encourage visual aids and hands-on experiences; teach active reading (underlining), active listening (note taking, repeating what you've said), reading for detail (questioning techniques), and subvocalizing (whispering) to aid memory and attention. Take advantage of challenging moments to discuss what you're thinking and what your child is thinking. Look for agreement points.

Monitor Progress Closely

One problem with current AD/HD treatment is that those who diagnose AD/HD and those who implement and monitor treatment may not be in close communication. Use a team approach in diagnosing and treating children with AD/HD. As your child's most important advocate, you must deal with both the medical and educational system to ensure appropriate services and follow up. Get familiar with your child's educational and legal rights and actively participate in her/his education. Federal disability laws mandate educational accommodations be available for children with AD/HD, and modifications in public-school settings can be as important to your child's treatment as medical intervention.

Strategies for Change

- Hold family meetings to discuss the week's events, challenges, and unresolved issues. Encourage family members to add items of discussion to the list as they occur during the week.

- When there is a problem, write it down for the clarification of both you and your child.

- Brainstorm some specific steps together to remedy the problem; have your child help determine what consequences ought to be for misbehaviors.

- Make use of memory strategies—lists, reminders, notes, and calendars.

- Provide frequent feedback, not just negative, but as much positive feedback as possible.

- Redirect, rather than command your child's attention.

- Encourage responsibility wherever and whenever possible.

- Consider using a coach or tutor to help your child with schoolwork.

- Explore what educational software programs might be available to help your child study independently and make meaningful connections.

- Provide your child with whatever devices or tools (e.g., calculator, computer software programs) she/he demonstrates help.

- Be consistent with rules and principles that you feel are most important. Be willing to let the less important battles be won by your child.

- Always remember to negotiate rather than fight or struggle.

Consult a Physician/Mental-Health Specialist

If your family doctor does not impress you as being knowledgeable on the subject, consider taking your child to a developmental pediatrician or a psychologist that specializes in AD/HD. Psychostimulants such as Ritalin/Concerta (methylphenidate), Adderall (amphetamine) and Dexedrine (dextroamphetamine) and some antidepressants are the most widely accepted medications for AD/HD. Many psychiatrists prefer the stimulant Adderall, since it has proven in some studies to be more effective than Ritalin/Concerta. However, no single AD/HD drug *always* works for every child, and doctors depend on the input of parents and teachers to find the most effective individual treatment. Sometimes a series of medications must be tried before a child's behavior improves and side effects are mitigated.

Treat Appropriately

Most students with *serious* forms of AD/HD do better in school once they are on appropriate medication combined with behavioral therapy (see Appendix for an example of a writing assignment before and after AD/HD medications). Behavioral therapy alone has been shown in some studies to be effective in treating severe AD/HD behaviors/symptoms. Before your child is caught up in a negative failure cycle at school, provide extra preparation for their entry into the classroom. AD/HD medications should be reserved for the last line of defense and should rarely be given to children younger than six years old.

Seek Support

This can be a frustrating time for everyone in the family. Remember to be patient and understanding with your AD/HD child and

Students with AD/HD can succeed if parents and teachers help them learn how to deal with their problems and overcome their limitations.

other family members. Talking to other parents or getting involved with a support group, such as Children and Adults With Attention-Deficit Disorder, through your local hospital may be helpful. Check in regularly with your child's teacher to get a reading on daily behaviors. Also seek a consultation with a health professional to rule out other possible psychological problems, such as depression or a learning disorder.

Cooperate with School Personnel

Conference with your child's teacher (and other school personnel) regularly. Try to ascertain the teacher's experience level and philosophical approach to AD/HD. If you wish to get more information or are concerned that the teacher is not able to work with your child effectively, consult the school nurse, school psychologist, or principal. Be sure that school personnel know what medication (if any) your child is taking, and inform them of the approach you're using at home so that it can be reinforced at school. Agree on appropriate rules and consequences and be consistent with them at home.

Checklist for School Preparedness

✓ *Design a Personalized Behavior Program:* Target a few unacceptable behaviors with clear consistent consequences that are fully understood and agreed upon by your child. Consequences should <u>not</u> be humiliating, threatening, or physically violent (i.e., spanking).

✓ *Role Model Effective Organizational Skills:* Encourage children to use planning techniques, such as a daily planner, computer software program, or a simple notebook.

✓ *Modify the Environment:* Request that your child be seated near the front of the classroom. Remind his/her teacher that your child does best when given plenty of time to engage in tactile stimulation and manipulation activities. Request that your child be allowed to request a break or to stand in the back of the room when necessary.

✓ *Reinforce Self-Esteem:* Encourage mastery in your child's areas of strength and personal interest; provide plenty of feedback and positive reinforcement. Redirect rather than command.

✓ *Encourage Active Learning:* Use visual aids, hands-on experiences, and group processes when possible to engage the AD/HD brain. Teach study skills, such as reading with a highlighter (underlining), active listening (note taking), reading for detail, summarizing, and memory "tricks" such as sub-vocalizing (whispering) to aid memory and attention.

✓ *Repeat and Remind:* Repeat important information a number of times. Remind your child to consult their notebooks and planning calendars at the end of class to ensure necessary materials for homework are brought home.

✓ *Be Consistent:* This is especially important for things like homework expectations, rules and policies, and scheduled activities and routines.

7 *Solutions for Teachers*

One can either ignore, accommodate, or treat the AD/HD student. For most classroom teachers, the appropriate role is accommodation. Ignoring the problem is a bad choice. Students with minor AD/HD symptoms may never be diagnosed with the condition, but the teacher who recognizes that a student is struggling can use simple accommodations to ensure their success. More severe AD/HD is likely to be diagnosed and an Individual Education Plan (IEP) created.

Not every child with AD/HD requires the same accommodation. Variations in brains produce variations in specific abilities in various environments. Biological problems can have simple environmental solutions. The severity of symptoms and the child's particular situation need to be considered before establishing a treatment plan. The primary purpose of any modification should be to teach the child with AD/HD the mechanisms for coping with their condition. The basic accommodations teachers learn to make for the AD/HD learner, such as reducing distractions, providing consistent structure, chunking instructions, and teaching memory strategies, benefit all students, in fact. Knowing when to be flexible, when to accommodate, and when to increase structure represents the subtlety that makes the science of teaching a true art form. Every student, not just those with AD/HD, will benefit from your good contingency-management skills and planning.

Empower with Skill Development

Although it is important to provide the AD/HD learner with consistent support and accommodation, it is equally important to avoid pampering or unconsciously allowing behaviors that are detrimental to learning. For example, it is productive to provide an extension and extra support on a project in which the AD/HD learner is truly facing a learning challenge; however, it is counterproductive to extend the deadline because the student informs you at the eleventh hour that he/she couldn't do it because it was too difficult. In other words, don't encourage excuse making, but also don't discourage the sincere request for additional help. A fine line divides these actions, but if you know your students well enough, you will sense when they are seeking a hand out versus a hand up.

Students who learn they can use their condition to excuse themselves are not being well served. Over time, a pattern of "learned helplessness" can develop in which the student truly believes he/she cannot accomplish what others can because of his/her condition. Eventually this student stops trying. Remember, the number one goal is to teach the AD/HD student the tools that will help him/her *succeed* in school, not fail. The key is to empower students so they can better manage their own life. Show them they can adapt to adversity and succeed no matter what the challenge.

Focus on Strengths and Provide Support

Understanding the condition and knowing how to accommodate the AD/HD student are essential. If you are a *new* teacher, the challenge will be greater: You will have more on your plate and your stress level may be higher. But remember, the best way to manage AD/HD students effectively is to provide a positive learning environment that focuses on strengths, rather than weaknesses. Provide extra support wherever needed. Adjustments—*both* physical, environmental, and to your curriculum—may be necessary to achieve the appropriate challenge level for the AD/HD learner. The more focus given to what's wrong, the greater the disservice to the child. We all have our weaknesses; it is our strengths, however, that help us thrive in the world.

Accommodate, Accommodate, Accommodate

Trying to fix or cure the AD/HD student is counterproductive. They are not broken: Rather, they need understanding and accommodation. It is not necessary for every child in the classroom to receive identical assignments. What *is* necessary is that every student receives the appropriate support and accommodation to ensure the target learning occurs. Maintain a positive attitude with these students and recognize their inherent struggle. Balance the amount of direction and structure you provide with a healthy quantity of responsibility and opportunities for self-empowerment. Be flexible, but maintain consistent boundaries on important issues, such as those that involve their own and others' safety and the establishment of productive learning habits.

Use a Behavioral-Modification Approach

Focus on reinforcing positive behaviors and channeling negative ones. Behavior modification is most effective when done immediately at the

time the behavior occurs. If you attend to it later, AD/HD learners aren't likely to internalize the information. Obviously, you can't always be at the student's side, but you can create an infrastructure that provides consistent support as much as possible (e.g., star charts, extra privileges, self-assessment checklists, cooperative teams, partner grading, multiple feedback mechanisms, etc.). Pinpoint one or two behaviors to modify at a time so that the student (and you) don't become overwhelmed. Choose your battles carefully. Use positive affirmations!

Avoid Threats and Stress

Too much pressure can cause the AD/HD brain to shut down and underperform. This is why a gentle and moderate approach is best. Rather than making threats like "If you don't stop talking, you're going to lose points or have to stay after school," say something like, "Let's set three goals that we want to accomplish today. In five minutes, I'll check back with you to see if you're on track." Never embarrass a student for his/her AD/HD behavior. It is not their choice: They have a condition. These students are different, but then again, aren't we all in one way or another?

Provide Immediate External Reinforcement

Since the AD/HD student has a much harder time with delaying gratification than the average student, provide plenty of *immediate* feedback and external motivators. Good motivation tools include a point system, a star chart, peer approval, extra recognition, and modification of responsibilities and/or privileges. Acknowledge progress, goal achievement, and appropriate behaviors. Encourage parents to use similar motivators.

Establish Routines and Provide Structure

Create high predictability through daily and weekly events that always happen on cue. For example, provide a daily overview of the lesson plan; open class the same way each time; transition from one activity to the next in a routine way; end class with a predictable closure; and make one or more days out of the week special in some way (e.g., Monday "Goal Setting" Session, Wednesday "Check-In" Session, and Friday "Celebration Time"). When the routine varies, acknowledge the change. Structure relieves the AD/HD brain of the hassle, challenge, and temporal decisions needed to continually readjust and accommodate change.

Incorporate More Movement

Keep your classroom active and encourage a daily school-supported physical education program. Include plenty of movement and hands-on activities in your lessons. Vary the types of movements from sitting to standing to walking to running. To control inappropriate behaviors, limit "free" time. Establish a signal system that the AD/HD student understands so that communication between you and him/her can be either verbal or non-verbal. A signal should be agreed upon that indicates to the student that it is time to take a "break." Allow students to sit or stand at the back of the room so they can move around without disturbing others.

> *Trying to fix or cure the AD/HD student is counterproductive. They are not broken: Rather they need understanding and accommodation.*

Sharpen Communication

Important information such as ground-rules, grading policies, assignments, team/group divisions, upcoming events, etc. should be written down and posted in obvious locations in the room. Make it as easy as possible for the AD/HD learner to access information. Keep oral instructions brief and repeat them; provide written instructions (and review them orally) for multi-step processes; and divide learning tasks and homework into multiple steps with mini-milestones built in. Keep key information on the chalkboard or flipchart and teach students to use an organizer and refer to it often.

Manage Information Flow

Teach learners how to manage information so that they don't become overwhelmed. Show them how to scan and review reading material, how to focus on first and last sentences and paragraphs, and how to break tasks into chunks. In small groups, students can create their own checklists of key action items to be completed. Provide helpful self-check criteria and/or daily checklists; show them how to proof their work before turning it in; help them set up a planning calendar or note-book (i.e., listing homework assignments and due dates; textbooks/supplies needed, etc.). Write instructions out for them, and repeat important information. Teach them memory tricks (mnemonics) like writing key words in the air and associating something they want to remember with a silly or novel visual image.

Increase Feedback

AD/HD students rarely plan for the future or reflect on the past. They live in the moment more often than not. Do not expect them to manage goals and dreams in their head for long. Capture the moment with the use of activities that provide instant feedback like:

- ☞ **Self-checking rubrics**
- ☞ **Group and team charts**
- ☞ **Games and friendly competition**
- ☞ **Peer editing**
- ☞ **Arts and hands-on activities**
- ☞ **Computers (if age appropriate)**
- ☞ **Gallery walks**
- ☞ **Discussion and brainstorming**

Focus on the student's strengths and successes. Acknowledge even partial progress. Don't wait until mastery is achieved to praise them. Use external motivators like progress charts and point systems, where good behavior earns points towards classroom privileges. Incorporate group activities to increase peer feedback. Monitor procrastination tendencies by establishing mini-milestones with the child.

Teach Time-Management Skills

Teach students how to break up learning tasks into chunks and manage them with an external reminder system (i.e., planning calendar, notes, computer programs, etc.). Help students manage their time in the classroom with prompts, pointers, timers, bells, and timekeepers. Be sure to allot time expectations to assignments and requests so that there are no surprises. Provide ample warning when a transition from one activity to another is about to occur. A buddy system can sometimes reduce impulse-control problems and provide additional support for the AD/HD student.

Make Classroom Space More Functional

Consider creating stations in the classroom for various functions—for example, where students can go to read or write without distraction, listen to soothing music, or work with manipulatives. At the very least, provide a cozy "student office" space where working quietly and independently is encouraged. Room dividers, storage cabinets, bookcases, or simple plastic boxes can be easily adapted for this purpose.

Involve the Entire Class

Hold class meetings and address behavior topics that are especially relevant to AD/HD, such as respect, breaking bad habits, problem solving, noise levels, etc., Be careful not to single out the AD/HD student. You might introduce a topic or theme each Monday that will be addressed throughout the week. Facilitate a discussion about how it feels to be disrespected, interrupted, or bullied by others. To be maximally effective, introduce only one topic at a time and revisit the topic on various occasions.

Refer Out as Necessary

If you suspect your AD/HD student may have a comorbid or overlapping condition, consult with his/her parents and refer to the school psychologist and/or other

The basic accommodations teachers can make for the AD/HD learner, such as reducing distractions, providing consistent structure, chunking instructions, and teaching memory strategies, benefit all students, in fact.

medical/mental-health professional. This is your call and it's an important one. Ask yourself, "Can I handle this student? Am I skilled enough? Is the student otherwise healthy and happy?" If the answers are yes, classroom accommodations may be enough to manage the student without medical intervention. If, however, the answer to any of these questions is no, then seek the appropriate help.

Accommodation Tips

- ✏ Use a timer to help learners monitor their time; provide strategies for self-monitoring.

- ✏ Increase immediacy of rewards and consequences; praise appropriate behavior.

- ✏ Don't penalize learners for poor handwriting if visual-motor deficits are present.

- ✏ Encourage the use of memory helpers such as a day planner, notebooks, memo boards, and reminder notes; supervise the recording of homework assignments to reduce confusion at home.

- ✏ Incorporate previewing strategies and review tips; teach learners the importance of repetition to the brain.

- ✏ Give students the option of standing, getting a drink, or taking a fast walk around the parameter of the room when necessary.

Checklist for Teacher Success

✓ Place the AD/HD learner in a quiet place with few distractions when concentration is required.

✓ Assign one task at a time; break large tasks into multiple smaller tasks and set mini-milestones.

✓ Encourage list-making and other memory strategies.

✓ Stick to routines and provide structure throughout the day.

✓ Focus on the child's strengths; give credit even if the ultimate goal has yet to be reached.

✓ Avoid arguing and no-win discussions; pick your battles.

✓ Set fair limits and stick to them; no negotiating.

✓ Avoid punishment/taking away privileges as the primary reinforcement; use positive discipline methods such as redirection and mini breaks to reorient.

✓ Role model healthy behaviors; be organized yourself; avoid using substances for coping with stress; get enough sleep, recreation, and exercise. Keep a positive attitude.

✓ Walk your students through complex tasks; ask key questions; and let them know you are there for support when they need it.

✓ Avoid unrealistic expectations (e.g., to remember a five-step sequence of directions).

✓ Develop your contingency-management skills; always have a plan A, B, and C, and remain flexible and calm when faced with the unexpected.

✓ Maintain clear daily, weekly, and monthly lesson plans and goals; help learners create their own personal goals, as well.

✓ Always use a loving approach, despite the frustrations.

✓ Encourage healthy peer relationships; provide guidance on how to be a good friend to others.

✓ Celebrate appropriately when a performance goal is reached.

Empower with
Skill Development

Focus on Strengths/
Provide Support

Establish
Routines/Provide
Structure

Accommodate

Provide Immediate
External
Reinforcement

Incorporate
Movement

**Solutions
for
Teachers**

Avoid Threats
& Stress

Use a Behavioral-
Modification
Approach

Make Classroom
Space More
Functional

Involve the
Entire Class

Sharpen
Communication

Manage
Information Flow

Teach Time-
Management Skills

Refer Out as
Necessary

Putting It All Together

✏ If you suspect a learner may have AD/HD, speak to the parents and refer them to the school psychologist or other medical/mental-health professional without delay. Remember, AD/HD is a spectrum disorder that can range in symptoms from mild to severe. The best treatment plan takes the degree of impairment or challenge exhibited by the child into account. Always start with appropriate accommodations.

☞ Combine learning with stimulating movement, music, and memory strategies including dance, stretching, cross-laterals, and rhythm in the classroom. The first three steps in treating AD/HD are accommodation; accommodation; accommodation. As a first line of defense, make classroom accommodations for the AD/HD learner and ask parents to work with you to come up with a behavioral learning plan that will be supported both at home and at school.

☞ A behavioral learning plan might include: (1) making the consequences of the child's actions more frequent and immediate; (2) increasing the external use of prompts and cues about rules and time intervals; (3) anticipating events for the AD/HD child or adult; (4) breaking future tasks down into smaller and more immediate steps; (5) reducing competition; (6) increasing support and structure; and (7) teaching self responsibility, initiative, and follow through by *not* doing a child's work for them.

☞ Avoid threat and stress. Too much pressure can shut the AD/HD brain down. When medium to high focus is required, arrange AD/HD learners in an area with the fewest distractions. Provide immediate and regular feedback on task performance.

☞ Learn all you can about current treatments for AD/HD. Remember, no single treatment option or prescription works well for every child, and doctors depend on the input of teachers and parents for establishing an effective individualized treatment plan.

☞ Children under the age of six should not be prescribed psychostimulants, such as Ritalin, Concerta, or Adderall. Non-drug alternatives need to be exhausted before resorting to a prescription drug. However, if there is consensus among physicians and parents that drug therapy is necessary, be aware that a series of drugs may have to be tried before a child's behavior improves and side effects are mitigated.

☞ To maximize focus and task performance, make sure AD/HD learners stay within the required daily dosage range of prescribed medications.

☞ Stay abreast of the latest news in this quickly changing area. New non-stimulant drugs are on the horizon, as well as potential tools for a more definitive AD/HD diagnosis.

We all have our weaknesses; it is our strengths, however, that help us thrive in the world.

Appendix I: Working Model of AD/HD

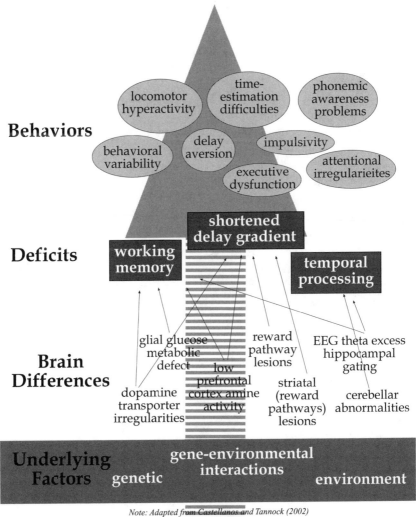

Note: Adapted from Castellanos and Tannock (2002)

Appendix II: Student Writing Samples

A Sample of an AD/HD Student's Paper <u>Before</u> Starting Medication

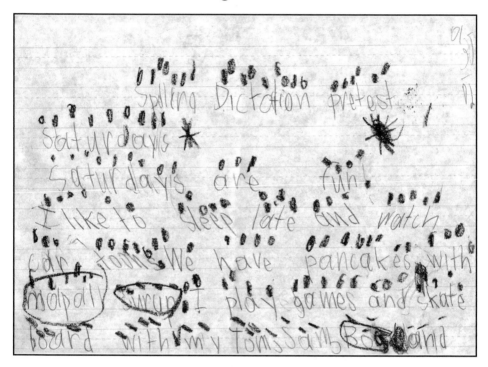

Tristin (2nd Grade) exhibited severe AD/HD symptoms. After a thorough diagnosis and series of alternative treatments and accommodations, he was prescribed methylphenidate by his physician. His school performance, as depicted by the "post-test" writing sample on the following page, immediately improved.

Tristin's Writing Sample <u>After</u> Starting Medication

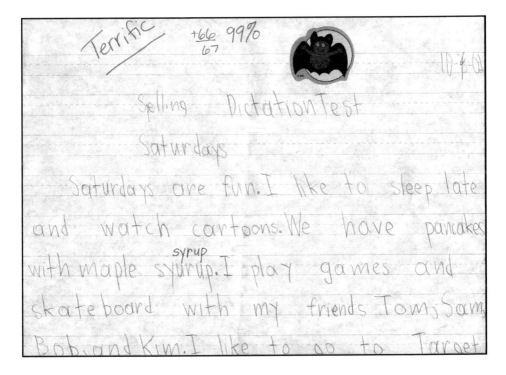

On the back of Tristin's "post-test," he still doodled, but rather than a bunch of circles and blots, he penned a couple of elaborate race cars.

Appendix III: Bibliography

American Medical Association. 1998. *Journal of the American Medical Association,* Council
  Report, April 8; 279(14):http://jama.ama-assn.org/issues/v279n14/abs/jcn71008.html#aainfo
American Psychiatric Association. 2000. *Diagnostic and Statistical Manual of Mental
  Disorders;* Fourth Edition, Text Revision. Washington, DC: American Psychiatric
  Association.
Arcia, E.; C.K. Conners. 1998. Gender differences in AD/HD? *Journal of
  Developmental and Behavioral Pediatrics.* 19: 77-83.
Barkley, R.A. 1998. Gene linked to AD/HD verified. *AD/HD Reports.* June; 6(3).
Barkley, R.A.; K.R. Murphy; and K.D. Kwasni. 1996. Motor vehicle driving
  competencies: Risks in teens and young adults with Attention-Deficit/Hyperactivity
  Disorder. *Pediatrics.* Dec; 98(6)-Pt 1: 1089-95.
Berman, T; V.I. Douglas; R.G. Barr. 1999. Effects of methylphenidate on complex
  cognitive processing in attention-deficit hyperactivity disorder; *J Abnorm Psychol.*
  Feb; 108(1): 90-105. Department of Psychology, McGill University, Montreal,
  Quebec, Canada.
Barbaresi, William, et al. 2002. How common is AD/HD? *Archives of Pediatrics and
  Adolescent Medicine.* Mar; 156(3) 217-24.
Barry, Robert, et al. EEG coherence in AD/HD: A comparative study of two DSM-IV
  TR types. *Clinical Neurophysiology.* 113(4): 579-85.
Biederman, Joseph, et al. 2002. Influence of gender on AD/HD in children referred to a
  psychiatric clinic. *Am J Psychiatry.* Jan; 159: 36-42.
Biederman, J.; E. Mick; S. Faraone. 2000-a. Age-dependent decline of AD/HD
  symptoms. *Int J of Neuropsychopharmacol.* 3(suppl 1): S60.
Biederman, J., et al. 2000-b. *American Journal of Psychiatry.* 157(5): 816-18.
Breggin, Peter. 2001. *Talking Back to Ritalin.* Cambridge, MA: Perseus Books.
Brook, et al. 2000. *Patient Education & Counseling.* 40(3): 247-52.
Brue, A.W., Oakland,T.D. 2002. Alternative treatments for AD/HD: Does evidence
  support their use? *Alternative Therapies.* Jan/Feb; 8(1): 68-74.
Campbell, L.; M.A. Malone; J.R. Kershner, et al. 1996. Methylphenidate slows right
  hemisphere processing in children with Attention-Deficit/Hyperactivity Disorder. *J
  Child Adolesc Psychopharmacol.* Winter; 6(4): 229-39. Department of Pediatrics,
  Hospital for Sick Children, University of Toronto.
Castellanos, Xavier, Patti Lee, Wendy Sharp, et al. 2002. Developmental trajectories of
  brain volume abnormalities in children and adolescents with Attention-
  Deficit/Hyperactivity Disorder. Journal of American Medical Association. 288(14).
  http://jama.ama-assn.org
Castellanos, Xavier, et al. 2001. Quantitative brain magnetic resonance imaging in girls
  with AD/HD. *Arch Gen Psychiatry.* Mar; 58(3): 289-95.
Castellanos, F.; R. Tannock. 2001 Neuroscience of Attention-Deficit/Hyperactivity
  Disorder: The search for endophenotypes. *Nature Reviews Neuroscience.* 3(8): 617-28.
Cherland and Fitzpatrick. 1999. Psychotic side effects of psychostimulants: A 5-year
  review. *Canadian Journal of Psychiatry.* Oct. 44: 811-13.
Clinical Courier. 2002. The Changing Face of AD/HD: A Focus on Current Trends in
  Disease Management. SynerMed Communications. Mar; 20(5).
Clure, et al. 1999. *American Journal of Drug and Alcohol Abuse.* 25(3): 441-8.
Colquhoun, Irene. 1994. Attention-Deficit/Hyperactive Disorder: A dietary nutritional
  approach. *Therapeutic Care & Education.* Summer; 3(2): 159-72.
Curran, et al. 1999. *American Journal of Psychiatry.* 156(10): 1664-5.
DeWolfe, N., et. al. 2000. *Journal of Attention Disorders.* 4(2): 80-90.
  Diagnostic and Statistical Manual of Mental Disorders (4th Edition) Text Revision.
  2000. Washington, DC: American Psychiatric Association.

Ding, Yuan-Chun, et al. 2002. Evidence of positive selection acting at the human dopamine receptor D4 gene locus. *Proc Nat Acad Sciences USA.* Jan; 99(1): 309-14.

Dougherty, D.D.; A.A. Bonab; T.J. Spencer, et al. 1999. Dopamine transporter density in patients with AD/HD. *The Lancet.* Dec; 354(9196): 2132-3.

Drug Information Handbook for Nursing. 1999. Turkowki, B.B. (Ed). Cleveland, OH: Lexi-Comp Inc.

Dunnick, J.K.; J.R. Hailey. 1995. Experimental studies on the long-term effects of methylphenidate hydrochloride; *Toxicology.* Nov 30; 103(2): 77-84. National Institute of Environmental Health Sciences, Research Triangle Park, NC 27709.

Dykman, Kathryn and Roscoe Dykman. 1998. Effect of nutritional supplements on Attentional-Deficit Hyperactivity Disorder. *Integrative Physiological & Behavioral Science.* 33 (1): 49-60.

Eghbalieh, B., et al. 2000. *Journal of Attention Disorders* 4(1): 5-13.

Eisenberg J; G. Mei-Tal; A. Steinberg, et al. 1999. Haplotype relative risk study of catechol-O-methyltransferase (COMT) and attention-deficit hyperactivity disorder (AD/HD): Association of the high-enzyme activity Val allele with AD/HD impulsive-hyperactive phenotype. *Am J Med Genetics.* Oct 15; 88(5): 497-502.

Ernst, M.; A.J. Zametkin; R.L. Phillip; R.M. Cohen. 1998. Age-related changes in brain glucose metabolism in adults with Attention-Deficit/Hyperactivity Disorder and control subjects. *Journal of Psychiatry and Clinical Neurosciences.* 104(2): 168-77.

Faraone, S.V.; A.E. Doyle. 2000. Genetic influences on Attention-Deficit Hyperactivity Disorder. Current Psychiatry Report. 2: 143-6.

Fletcher, P.; C. Buchel; O. Josephs; K. Friston, R. Dolan. 1999. Learning-related neuronal responses in prefrontal cortex studied with functional neuroimaging. *Cerebral Cortex.* March: 9(2): 168-78.

Funk, J.B.; J.B. Chessare; M.T. Weaver, et al. 1993. Attention-Deficit/Hyperactivity Disorder, creativity, and the effects of methylphenidate. *Pediatrics.* Apr; 91(4): 816-19.

Gadow, K.D.; J. Sverd; J. Sprafkin, et al. *Long-term Methylphenidate Therapy In Children with Co-morbid Attention-Deficit Hyperactivity Disorder and Chronic Multiple Tic Disorder.* Department of Psychiatry and Behavioral Science, State University of New York at Stony Brook, 11794-8790.

Goldman, L.S.; M. Genel; R.J. Bezman, P.J. Slanetz. 1998. Diagnosis and treatment of Attention-Deficit/Hyperactivity Disorder in children and adolescents. Council on Scientific Affairs; American Medical Assn. JAMA. 279: 1100-7.

Gruber, Reute; Avi Sadeh; Amiram Raviv. 2000. Instability of sleep patterns in children with AD/HD. *Journal of the American Academy of Child and Adolescent Psychiatry.* 39(4): 495-501.

(The) Harvard Mahoney Neuroscience Institute Letter. 2001. Present and future treatment of AD/HD. Spring/Summer; 8(2): 1-3.

Hitzeman, Robert. 2002. Personal communication, Portland, OR. His research specializes in substance abuse.

Jonkman, L.M.; C. Kemner; M.N. Verbaten, et al. 1997. Effects of methylphenidate on event-related potentials and performance of attention-deficit hyperactivity disorder children in auditory and visual selective attention tasks. Biol Psychiatry. Mar 15; 41(6): 690-702. Institute for Neurosciences, Utrecht University, The Netherlands.

Kastner, J., et al. 2000. *Psychology in the Schools.* 37(4): 367-77.

Kennerly, Patrick; John Markowitz. 1997. Pharmacology of methylphenidate enantiomers and pemoline in AD/HD. *Human Psychopharmacology Clinical & Experimental.* 12(6): 527-46.

Leroux & Levitt-Perlman. 2000. *Roeper Review.* 22(3): 171-6.

Lorch, et al. 2000. *Journal of Abnormal Psych.* 109(2): 321-30.

Marx, J. 1999. How stimulant drugs may calm hyperactivity. *Science.* Jan 15; 283(5400): 306.

Michelson, David, et al. 2001. Atomoxetine in the treatment of children and adolescents with AD/HD: A randomized, placebo-controlled, dose-response study. *Pediatrics.* Nov; 108(5): e83.

Mick, Eric, et al. 2002. Case control study of AD/HD and maternal smoking, alcohol use, and drug use during pregnancy. J Am Acad Child Adolesc Psychiatry. Apr; 41(4): 378-85.

Mick, Eric, et al. 2002. Impact of low birth weight on AD/HD. *J. Dev Behav Pediatr.* Feb; 23(1): 16-22.

Millstein, R.B.; T.E. Wilens; J. Biederman; T.J. Spencer. 1998. Presenting AD/HD symptoms and subtypes in clinically referred adults with AD/HD. *Journal of Attention Disorders.* 2: 159-66.

Molina, et al. 1999. *Psychology Addictive Behaviors.* 13(4): 348-58.

Monastra,Vincent, Lubar, Joel, Linden, Michael. 2001. The Development of a quantitative electroencephalographic scanning process for AD/HD: Reliability and validity studies. *Neuropsychology.* 15(1): 136-44.

MTA Cooperative Group. 1999. *Archives of General Psychiatry.* 56: 1073-86.

National Institute of Health (NIH). 2002. www.nlm.nih.gov/medlineplus/druginfo/uspdi/

Nolan, E.E.; K.D. Gadow; J. Sprafkin. 1999. Stimulant medication withdrawal during long-term therapy in children with comorbid Attention-Deficit/Hyperactivity Disorder and chronic multiple tic disorder. *Pediatrics.* Apr; 103 (4 Pt 1): 730-7. Department of Psychiatry and Behavioral Science, SUNY at Stony Brook, Stony Brook, New York 11794-8790.

Norvilitus, et al. 2000. *Journal of Attention Disorders.* 4(1): 15-26.

Peigneux, P.; S. Laureys; X. Delbeuck; P. Maquet. 2001. Sleeping brain, learning brain: The role of sleep for memory systems. *Neuroreport.* 12a: 111-24.

Phalen, Kathleen. 2002. World of distraction. *American Medical News.* Mar; 45(11): 24-5.

Rappley, Marsha D. 1999. Too many drugs for toddlers diagnosed with AD/HD. *Archives of Pediatric and Adolescent Medicine.* Oct; 153, Michigan State University.

Robison, L.M., et al. 2002. Is AD/HD increasing among girls in the US?: Trends in diagnosis and the prescribing of Stimulants. *CNS Drugs.* 16(2): 129-39.

Rowland, Andrew, et al. 2002. Prevalence of medication treatment for AD/HD among elementary school children in Johnston County, North Carolina. *Am J of Public Health.* Feb; 92(2): 231-4.

Rucklidge, J.J.; B.J. Kaplan. 1997. Psychological functioning of women identified in adulthood with Attention- Deficit/Hyperactivity Disorder. *Journal of Attention Disorders.* 2: 167-76.

Rucklidge, J.J.; R. Tannock. 2001. Psychiatric, psychosocial, and cognitive functioning of female adolescents with ADHD. *J Am Acad Child Adolesc Psychiatry.* May; 40(5): 530-40.

Sachs, G., et al. 2000. *American Journal of Psychiatry.* 157(3): 466-8.

Schachar, et al. 2000. *Journal of Abnormal Child Psychology.* 28(3): 227-35.

Segal, David; Ronald Kuczenski. 1999. Escalating dose-binge treatment with methylphenidate: Role of serotonin in the emergent behavioral profile. *Journal of Pharmacology & Experimental Therapeutics.* Oct; 291(1): 19-30. dsegal@ucsd.edu. Department of Psychiatry, School of Medicine, University of California at San Diego, La Jolla, CA, 92121.

Semrud-Clikeman, M.; J. Biederman; S. Sprich-Buckminister, et al. 1992. Comorbidity between AD/HD and learning disabilities: A review and report in a clinically referred sample. *Journal of the American Academy of Child and Adolescent Psychiatry.* 31(3): 439-48.

Shen, Roh-Yu, et al. 1999. Chronic ethanol, dopamine electrophysiology and craving. *Clinical & Experimental Research.* Nov; (23).

Sherman, Carl. 2002. Mathylphenidate not ideal for preschool AD/HD. *Clinical Psychiatry News.* Mar; 30(3): 16.

Smalley, S.L. 1997. Genetic influences in childhood-onset psychiatric disorders: Autism and Attention-Deficit/Hyperactivity Disorder. *American Journal of Human Genetics.* 60: 1276-82.

Sonuga-Barke, E.J. 2002. Psychological heterogeneity in AD/HD: A dual pathway model of behavior and cognition. *Behavioral Brain Research.* 130: 29-36.

Spencer, T; J. Biederman; T. Wilens. 1998. Growth deficits in children with AD/HD. *Pediatrics.* Aug; 102(2 Pt 3): 501-6. Department of Pediatric Psychopharmacology, Massachusetts General Hospital, Boston, Massachusetts 02114.

Stein, Mark. 1999. Unravelling sleep problems in treated and untreated children with AD/HD. *Journal of Child and Adolescent Psychopharmacology.* 9(3): 157-68.

Swanson, J.M.; S. Wigal; L.I. Greenhill, et al. 1998. Analog classroom assessment of Adderall in children with AD/HD. *Journal of the American Academy of Child and Adolescent Psychiatry.* 37: 519-26.

Thunstrom, M. 2002. Severe sleep problems in infancy associated with subsequent development of AD/HD at 5.5 years of age. *Acta Paediatrica.* 91(5): 584-92.

University of Wisconsin Medical School and Colwood Healthworld study through an unrestricted educational grant from McNeil Consumer and Specialty Pharmaceuticals. 2001. *Review of Recent Scientific Presentations on AD/HD: Advancing AD/HD Management and Treatment.* Nov. 23.

Vaidya, C.J.; G. Austin; G. Kirkorian; et al. Selective effects of methylphenidate in AD/HD: a functional magnetic resonance study. Department of Psychology, Stanford University, Stanford, CA 94305. vaidya@psych.stanford.edu.

Van Dyck, Christopher, et al. 2002. Unaltered dopamine transporter availability in adult AD/HD. *Am J Psychiatry.* Feb; 159(2): 309-12.

Vincent, J.; C.K. Varley; P. Leger. 1990. Effects of methylphenidate on early adolescent growth. *Am J Psychiatry.* Apr; 147(4): 501-2. Department of Psychiatry and Behavioral Sciences, University of Washington School of Medicine, Seattle.

Volkow, Nora; Gene-Jack Wang; Joanna S. Fowler, et al. 2001. Therapeutic doses of oral methylphenidate significantly increase extracellular dopamine in the human brain. *The Journal of Neuroscience.* 21(RC121): 1-5.

Volkow, Nora; Gene-Jack Wang; Joanna S. Fowler, et al. 1999. Reinforcing effects of psychostimulants in humans are associated with increase in brain dopamine and occupancy of D-sub-2 receptors. *Journal of Pharmacology & Experimental Therapeutics.* 291(1): 409-15.

Volkow, Nora; Gene-Jack Wang; Joanna S. Fowler, et al. 1998. Dopamine transporter occupancies in the human brain induced by therapeutic doses of oral methylphenidate. *American Journal of Psychiatry.* 155(10): 1325-31.

Volkow, N.D., et al. 1995. Is methylphenidate like cocaine? Studies on their pharmokinetics and distribution in the human brain. *Archives of General Psychiatry.* 52: 456-63.

Volkow, N.D.; G.J. Wang; J.S. Fowler, et al. 1996. Decreases in dopamine receptors but not in dopamine transporters in alcoholics. *Alcohol Clinical Experimental Research.* 20(9): 1594-8

Wender, P.H., et al. 2001. Adults with ADHD: An overview. *Ann NY Acad Sci.* 931: 1-16.

Wigg, Karen, et al. 2002. ADHD and the Gene for Dopamine Beta-Hydroxylase. *Am J Psychiatry.* June; 159(6): 1046-8.

Zakon, H.H. 1997. The effects of steroid cells on electrical excitabile cells. *Trends In Neuroscience.* 21(5): 202-7.

Appendix IV: Supplemental Resources

Websites

American Medical Association - www.ama-assn.org

Centers for Disease Control and Prevention - www.cdc.gov

Child Development Institute - www.cdipage.com or www.oneaddplace.com

Children and Adults With Attention-Deficit Disorder (CHADD) - www.chadd.org

National Attention-Deficit Disorder Association - www.add.org

National Institute of Health - www.nih.gov

Books

Attention Please!, by Edna Copland, PhD & Valerie Love, MEd

(The) ADD Hyperactivity Workbook for Parents, Teachers, & Kids, by Harvey Parker, PhD

Different Brains Different Learners, by Eric Jensen

Driven to Distraction, by Edward Hallowell, MD

(The) Gift of Dyslexia, by Ronald Davis

Healing AD/HD, by Daniel Amen

If I Could, I Would: A Teenager's Guide to Hyperactivity, by Michael Gordon

Natural Treatments for Hyperactivity, by Skye Weintraub

Raising Your Spirited Child, by Mary Sheedy Kurcinka

Reclaiming Our Children, by Peter Breggin, MD

Running on Ritalin, by Lawrence Diller, MD

Talking Back to Ritalin (Revised) by Peter Breggin, MD

Unraveling the ADD/ADHD Fiasco, by David Stein, PhD

Your Drug May Be Your Problem, by Peter Breggin, MD

About the Author

A former teacher and current member of the International Society for Neuroscience, **Eric Jensen,** has taught at all education levels, from elementary through university. In 1981 Jensen co-founded SuperCamp, the nation's first and largest brain-compatible learning program for teens, which now claims more than 25,000 graduates. He is currently President of Jensen Learning Corp. in San Diego, California. His other books include *Music with the Brain in Mind, Learning Smarter, Different Brains Different Learners, The Great Memory Book, Teaching with the Brain in Mind, Brain-Compatible Strategies, Sizzle and Substance, Trainer's Bonanza, Completing the Puzzle,* and *Super Teaching.* He's listed in Who's Who Worldwide and remains deeply committed to making a positive, significant, and lasting difference in the way the world learns. Jensen is a sought-after conference speaker who consults and trains educators in the U.S. and abroad. **The author can be contacted at eric@jlcbrain.com.**

Appendix VI: Index

CORWIN PRESS

The Corwin Press logo—a raven striding across an open book—represents the union of courage and learning. Corwin Press is committed to improving education for all learners by publishing books and other professional development resources for those serving the field of PreK–12 education. By providing practical, hands-on materials, Corwin Press continues to carry out the promise of its motto: **"Helping Educators Do Their Work Better."**